Racial Profiling in America

Racial Profiling in America

Alejandro del Carmen, Ph.D.
The University of Texas at Arlington

PEARSON
Prentice
Hall

Upper Saddle River, New Jersey 07458

1-7-2008
GBG
$41

Library of Congress Cataloging-in-Publication Data

Carmen, Alejandro del.
    Racial profiling in America / Alejandro del Carmen.— 1st ed.
      p. cm.
    ISBN-10: 0-13-114694-7 (alk. paper)
    ISBN-13: 978-0-13-114694-5 (alk. paper)
   1. Racial profiling in law enforcement—United States.   2. Discrimination in law enforcement—United States.
   3. Discrimination in criminal justice administration—United States.   I. Title.
    HV8141.C347 2008
    363.2'32—dc22

                              2007024283

Editor-in-Chief: Vernon R. Anthony
Senior Acquisitions Editor: Tim Peyton
Editorial Assistant: Alicia Kelly
Marketing Manager: Adam Kloza
Production Liaison: Joanne Riker
Cover Design Director: Jayne Conte
Cover Design: Bruce Kenselaar
Cover Images: James Gritz/Getty Images/Photodisc Green
Full-Service Project Management/Composition: Integra Software Services, Ltd.
Printer/Binder: Courier Companies Inc.,

Credits and acknowledgments borrowed from other sources and reproduced, with permission, in this textbook appear on appropriate page within text.

Pearson Education LTD.
Pearson Education Singapore, Pte. Ltd
Pearson Education, Canada, Ltd
Pearson Education–Japan

Pearson Education Australia PTY, Limited
Pearson Education North Asia Ltd
Pearson Educación de Mexico, S.A. de C.V.
Pearson Education Malaysia, Pte. Ltd

                    10 9 8 7 6 5 4 3 2 1
ISBN-13: 978-0-13-114694-5
ISBN-10:   0-13-114694-7

To Denise, Gabriel, and Gemma
and in loving memory of
Luisa Amaya
and Lt. Jeff Tucker

Contents

Chapter 3   Law Enforcement: Historical and Cultural Perspectives   *31*

Chapter 4   Civil Rights and Racial Profiling   *48*

Preface

As I write this book in the middle of another sizzling Texas summer, racial profiling continues to capture the public's attention in ways that perhaps just a few years ago, no one could have imagined. It could be argued that after the terrorist attacks of 9/11, racial profiling has become more relevant and timely than most social issues in the era of homeland security. Thus, it is safe to say that racial profiling is a major social issue currently affecting academics, practitioners, and members of our society focused on social justice issues.

This book is written with you in mind. That is, it is not a textbook filled with unsubstantiated arguments and selective citations. Rather, it is a reflection of racial profiling today, largely drawn from my experiences as an academic and a consultant to hundreds of police agencies in Texas. However, a word of caution is in order: This book is not a biographical sketch of my experiences or a series of personal interpretations of the areas I consider valuable in the racial profiling debate. Although I haven't shied away from presenting different points of view, it will be up to you to determine the information you consider most valuable. Clearly, my hope is to bring to light perspectives that you have not considered in the debate over racial profiling in the United States. You will notice that the book is written in a reader-friendly manner with a limited number of citations. The writing style and format of the book are meant to allow you to focus on the issues relevant to racial profiling without pedagogical distractions.

As I began to learn more about this topic some years ago, I quickly discovered that it was a heavily polarizing and divisive area where often individuals' feelings and beliefs were challenged. Thus, it is no easy task to write a book on this topic while remaining factual instead of emotional. I hope that in the early stages of this book, you will realize that the ways in which the racial profiling paradox can be resolved will not be provided; rather, you will be exposed to different philosophies or schools of thought that will provide some insights into this polarizing concept. The ultimate truth lies in you in the process of entertaining all of these different perspectives.

Although there are multiple definitions of racial profiling, most authors and experts alike agree that racial profiling constitutes, for the most part, the selective targeting of individuals based on their race, ethnicity, or religious affiliation. Although the concept is often used to describe police-initiated behavior, it also pertains to individuals who are in a position to target others based on their racial, ethnic, or religious background.

For purposes of this book, however, racial profiling will be referenced in the context of how this term applies to criminal justice agencies in general and law enforcement organizations in particular. The goal here is to relate racial profiling to the ongoing debate based on allegations that police officers target minority drivers based on variables other than traffic-related offenses.

While keeping up with the literature and legislative processes related to racial profiling, it became clear to me that it is difficult, if not impossible, to find a single book that presents a comprehensive view of this important and timely topic. In fact, I would argue that I have yet to find a book on racial profiling that has examined, in detail, the complexities of this particular issue. Most books on this topic focus on a particular aspect of profiling or perhaps introduce discussions on a few of the dilemmas surrounding racial profiling. Some authors have focused on legislation relevant to profiling, while others provide a detailed account of criminal profiling without making a clear distinction between this law enforcement technique and the act of making an unlawful traffic stop based on bias and racism .

Therefore, it is my hope that this book will address this shortcoming in the literature and serve as an outlet of information to educate the general public, particularly college students, on the topic of racial profiling. The topics introduced in this book were carefully selected in order to provide a comprehensive overview of the origins and components of racial profiling, and the dilemmas and challenges surrounding it. I would argue that this book is like no other focused on this topic as it introduces topics of discussion by the traditional academic approach while incorporating personal anecdotes related to specific aspects of a researcher's point of view.

Acknowledgments

This book would have never been written without the support and love of many individuals who have affected, in one way or another, different aspects of my life. I am particularly thankful to God for allowing me to have the focus, vision andstrength to complete this project. In addition, I am most grateful to my wife and children for their love and support which have carried me through the years. Having dedicated this book to them is but a small token of my appreciation.

I am also grateful to my parents, Alejandro and Maria Cristina, for their love and guidance. Their words of encouragement have been constant companions throughout my life. In addition, a special note of gratitude to Marcela and Mauricio for their love and support. I continue to find inspiration in Marcela as she provides her wonderful healing hands to so many patients who are in need of her love and care.

My academic formation is a result of many years of mentoring and guidance. Although many individuals have contributed to this process, I am particularly grateful to my colleagues and friends—John Stickels, Rhonda Dobbs, Elmer Polk, Caryl Segal, Robert Bing, Rob Sarver, Shannon Fowler, John Rodriguez, Rick Smith, Beth Wright, Randy Butler, Roberto Trevino, Dwight Steward, Susan Gonzales-Baker, Doug Richmond, , Helen Taylor-Greene, Rita Watkins, Cathy Moseley, Lindy Sprong and Pam Clark. Thank you for the contributions each of you have made to my formation as an academic in the field of criminology and criminal justice.

Throughout my tenure as an academic, students have often inspired me to carry out my role as a teacher and researcher in a more effective manner. Although I have had the privilege of interacting with many students during ten years of academic work, there are some whom I will never forget for they have left a mark in my life and have probably taught me more than I have ever contributed to their academic formation. These include Lacy Henderson, Ken Myers, Conrad Averna, Michael Ikner, Karel Carpenter, Bonnie Grohe, Michael Thomas, J.R. Price, Chris Copeland, Sara Mobley, Joshua Prescott, Chris Cook, Jacquelyn Lee, Brittany Rodriguez, Jacklyn Smith, Michele Whitehead, Chad Gann, Kendra Bowen, Natalie Sears, Chris McLucas, and Rebecca Wenzel.

I owe a great deal of gratitude to my editor, Margaret Lannamann. Margaret was always professional, kind, and encouraging throughout the process of writing, editing, and finalizing this manuscript. I benefited a great deal from her constructive criticisms and guidance. Also, a special note of gratitude to the LEMIT staff; particularly, Regina Guthrie.

Finally, I would like to express my appreciation to the reviewers—Dr. Rita Watkins, Sam Houston State University; Shaun L. Gabbidon, Penn State Harrisburg; Kevin Brogeson, Salem State; and Lori Guevara, Fayetteville State University—whose contributions and recommendations allowed me to produce a better-quality manuscript. I am also particularly grateful to the Prentice Hall team for allowing me to realize my dream of writing a book on racial profiling that would make a significant contribution to the existing body of knowledge. I am grateful to Frank Mortimer for his patience and belief in my abilities as a writer. I am very thankful to Tim Peyton, criminal justice editor for Prentice Hall, and Joanne Riker, who led the production team. I would also like to thank Kavitha Kuttikan and the team at Integra Software Services for their work on this book.

Throughout my academic career, I have met a large number of police professionals whom I have come to know and respect. Some of these include Chiefs Brett McGuire, Tom Cowan, Robert Gracia, Dallis Warren, Gary Swindle, Ralph Mendoza, Ron Echols, Brian Frieda, J.B. McCaleb, W. McManus and Bill Rushing.

This book is also dedicated to the memory of two very special people in my life—one of them is my grandmother, Luisa Amaya, who passed away last year. Her love and affection will forever remain in me. In so many ways, I have become a product of her love, care, and wisdom.

Also, Lt. Jeff Tucker, from the Rosenberg Police Department, passed away before the completion of this book. I met Jeff some years back and grew to respect him for his work ethics and constant concern for others. I will always specially remember him and, particularly, our conversations about racial profiling and different aspects of policing.

A final note of gratitude is in order for all my students whose names I have not included here. I thank you for allowing me to be part of your academic tenure. Keep up the good work and remember that "From those to whom much is given, much shall be required."

CHAPTER 1

Introduction to Racial Profiling

The concept of racial profiling has been in existence for years. In American history books, we find that profiling based on race was prevalent during the period of slavery. In fact, even during the early stages of the Jim Crow years (the 1890s), racial profiling was practiced. According to Davis (2005), the "Jim Crow Cars," otherwise known as segregated railroad cars, were in existence a few years before the early stages of the Jim Crow era. These segregated cars prompted blacks to ride in a separate module than their Caucasian counterparts. The notion that blacks were singled out by their racial makeup prompts us to argue that racial profiling was alive and well in the early stages of slavery in the United States.

THE JIM CROW ERA

The term *Jim Crow* is thought to have originated around 1830 when a "white, minstrel show performer, Thomas 'Daddy' Rice, blackened his face with charcoal paste or burnt cork and danced a ridiculous jig while singing lyrics to the song, 'Jump Jim Crow' " (Davis, 2005, p. 1). It is believed that Rice created this character after having witnessed, while in one of his travels in the South, a handicapped, elderly black man dancing and singing a song with these words:

> *Weel about and turn about and do jis so,*
> *Eb'ry time I weel about I jump Jim Crow* (Davis, 2005, p. 1)

This character became so popular that by the 1850s, "Jim Crow" became a main component of every minstrel show scene in the United States. As the Civil War neared, the concept of Jim Crow served as a stereotype image depicting blacks as inferior, in the popular culture in the United States. In fact, most historians agree that the words *Jim Crow* were often used as a racial slur to describe blacks.

Arguably, the Jim Crow era was not only a historical period when blacks were labeled with ridiculous names; it also constituted a period of time when the American culture was affected in a profound manner. First, it was affected to the extent that blacks became, as a matter of popular culture, identified and recognized as being inferior. Second, this era was known to have witnessed the enactment of laws that strengthened the segregation initiatives already in existence.

Some of the laws enacted during this era aimed at crippling the ability of blacks to move forward. For instance, the passing of laws prohibiting adult black males from voting was significant in that it disinherited blacks from having a basic Constitutional right already afforded to their Caucasian counterparts. In addition, blacks were obliged, as a matter of law, to segregate and simply live in separate areas of town from their Caucasian counterparts. Obviously, the separation was not only physical; instead, it also meant that Caucasians, unlike blacks, were able to enjoy improved social services provided by wealthier schools, churches, and hospitals.

Perhaps the most destructive feature of the Jim Crow era was the impact it had on the culture or psyche of people. That is, this era witnessed what is now considered to be one of the most significant series of acts involving collective violence that the United States has even known. These collective acts of violence, which were known as *lynchings*, were aimed for the most part at Southern blacks. According to Davis (2005), over 3,700 men and women were lynched in the United States from 1889 to 1930. Most of these individuals were Southern blacks. As you reflect on these numbers, keep in mind that hundreds if not thousands of lynchings took place during this era; most of which were never reported to local authorities or the media. In fact, the only riots that were recorded at the time were those initiated by white supremacists who were in favor of segregation and more lynchings.

The riots described earlier were not geographically limited to a specific area of the country per se. In fact, riots were recorded in cities ranging from Houston, Texas, to East St. Louis, to Tulsa, Oklahoma. It is reported that most of the riots that erupted at the time took place, for the most part, in urban areas of the country where Southern rural blacks had recently arrived. The level of violence was such that in a single summer (1919) numerous deaths and hundreds of injuries took place. This later became known as the *Red Summer of 1919* (Davis, 2005).

The underlying principle of the Jim Crow era specifically, and the slavery period generally, was that blacks were different from whites. That is, blacks were held to be inferior and of less intelligence than their counterparts. Thus, labeling of blacks as *Negroes* often occurred and became part of the existing culture. Stories were often produced (and manipulated) that would somehow confirm to a white audience that indeed blacks were inferior. These stories were based on "eyewitness" accounts of the filth, lack of morality, and absence of knowledge that seemed to be abundant in black households. In fact, they were often thought to speak an inappropriate version of English that was held as being a major deviation of proper conversational English.

All of these differentials gave rise to the concept of racial profiling. That is, the belief that due to the race of an individual the presence of social ailments was evident. For the most part, these social ailments (thought to be part of the black community) were often treated as a disease that would be easily communicable to others if not properly "treated." In other words, the concept of being proactive in ridding the world of such savage behavior was in order.

Clearly, this era of suspicion and labeling of blacks is not one of the proudest moments in American history. Sadly, most of us have discounted the impact of this era on the popular culture in existence today, which often "borrows" its inheritance from the Jim Crow years, as blacks become the "obvious" suspects in criminal investigations or perhaps the "likely" burglars roaming the affluent neighborhoods of a community. Thus, it is my contention that racial profiling, in its modern-day meaning, emerged during the Jim Crow era and has evolved throughout the years. This evolution, at times, has hidden the "essence" of the evil that lies in profiling while only presenting an "image" which appears to find harmony in the contemporary beliefs of equality and due process rights.

THE IMMIGRATION ERA

The concept of racial profiling was also present during the immigration era, when hundreds of thousands of immigrants arrived in the United States attempting to find a better way of life. Some of you may have heard the stories of your ancestors arriving on the shores of Boston or New York City while waving American flags at the sight of the Statue of Liberty. However, these Norman Rockwell images depicting the "American dream" quickly disappear when we discover in the history pages, records of laws excluding "certain" individuals, coupled with immigration officials labeling immigrants according to their country of origin, and their capacity to live healthy lives or engage in productive work.

According to Hutchinson (1981), the first federal act to authorize the exclusion of specific immigrant classes was the Act of 1875. This particular act aimed at prohibiting the entry to the United States of individuals who were suspected of being prostitutes or convicts. In fact, the first component of this act authorized consular officials in foreign posts, particularly in areas of the world where individuals from China, Japan, or any other Oriental nation were to depart to the United States, to determine if such travel was voluntary.

The rationale was to exclude all individuals who were determined to arrive in the United States by order of another party; that is, the idea was to prevent human trafficking. The Act of 1875 also provided for the imposition of penalties aimed at deterring individuals from bringing to the United States anyone deemed, by immigration officials, to be undesirable. The list of undesirables was long and complex, but it also included individuals whose lack of "moral" conviction could potentially endanger the apparent fragile moral ground in the United States.

The list of undesirables was heavily represented by individuals who originated from "certain" countries where wealth was scarce. In addition, it seems that individuals believed to be of "inferior" biological origins were also excluded from entering the United States. In fact, the Act of 1882 excluded not only the Chinese, but also individuals who were deemed as "lunatics" or "idiots." There were additional laws introduced throughout the years that provided the legal basis for the exclusion of undesirables. According to Abbott, in her book

Historical Aspects of the Immigration Problem, the individuals added to the exclusion list by these laws were:

> 1903—Polygamists and political radicals;
> 1907—Individuals with physical or mental defects and children that were not accompanied by their parents;
> 1917—Illiterates, persons of psychopathic inferiority, alcoholics, vagrants, women who intended to enter the country for immoral purposes, and stowaways.

It should be noted that stowaways could be admitted to the United States only at the discretion of the Secretary of Labor. The selective admission of these individuals suggests that the immigration policy generally, and the exclusion list specifically, was amended based on the needs of the labor market and economic conditions of the United States. Interestingly, the "label" given to these individuals, as part of a larger strategy to engage in profiling, was pervasive and did not change despite being allowed to enter the United States.

Once labeled as undesirables, immigrants were then deported. It is clear that deportation was also authorized by immigration laws as part of a larger strategy aimed at profiling and exterminating groups of immigrants thought to have the most significant predisposition to criminal activity. According to Hutchinson (1981), the U.S. Congress initially suggested the deportation of two broad types of cases. These involved aliens that had gained entry into the United States through some type of error in the screening process and those that, as a result of their "undesirable" behavior, had been issued the punishment of deportation. The first immigrant group to be declared by the U.S. Congress as being deportable was made up of individuals who were perceived as having the potential of "endangering" the new republic. In fact, the president of the United States was given the authority to expel "dangerous" aliens.

Despite the fact the presidential powers to expel aliens were authorized in the Aliens Act of June 25, 1798, Congress did not return to the issue of subversive activities until late in the nineteenth century, when the immigration of European anarchists gave rise to fear among U.S. officials. The fear was centered on the possibility that these individuals could engage in criminality or simply destroy the manner in which Americans lived their lives.

The point here is that immigration laws at the time used methods related to the modern notion of racial profiling in order to identify, classify, and deport individuals deemed as undesirables. Although the statutes read that the law pertained to individuals of questionable moral character or those that originated from specific countries (e.g., China), the idea was the same; that is, profile individuals of certain moral and character-related attributes by virtue of their racial background and deny them an opportunity to realize the "American dream." According to Hutchison (1981), legal mandates were in place to restrict the entry of individuals from the following groups:

a. Those unable to read or write in any language.
b. Unskilled workers unaccompanied by families.

To support this claim, I would like to direct the reader to the enactment of additional statutes at the time which aimed at implementing techniques meant to "weed out" individuals already identified as undesirable. These techniques utilized profiling while engaging in selective enforcement of the law in order to "make it difficult" for "certain" individuals to succeed. These statutes legalized the head tax, literacy test, quota system, and the suspension of immigration.

The first federal head tax was implemented as part of the Immigration Act of 1882. It established that each alien who arrived by steam or sail vessel from a foreign port had to pay the "modest" rate of 50 cents. Clearly, this particular requirement aimed at deterring individuals who were too poor to pay the fee or did not have anyone who would sponsor their intent to migrate to the United States. The fee soon escalated from 50 cents to 1 dollar in 1894. It was subsequently doubled to 2 dollars in 1903, while providing fee exemptions to individuals originating from specific countries such as Newfoundland. The head tax seems to have increased steadily and in 1952 it was set for 20 dollars per immigrant.

As mentioned earlier, another form of admission restriction of "certain" individuals was established by a statute that enabled the implementation of the literacy test. This particular test was originally suggested in 1891 by U.S. Congressman Henry Cabot Lodge. Congressman Lodge praised the test's effectiveness in excluding illiterate persons from being allowed residency in the United States. In fact, he argued when enacting the law, that it would be effective in preventing the admission of "all persons physically capable and over sixteen years of age who cannot read and write with reasonable facility their own language" (Lodge, 1891).

According to Hutchinson (1981), the implementation of the literacy test was effective in acting discriminately against the "most delinquent and pauper elements from abroad," while favoring northern and western Europeans. Despite this, the literacy test was well received as it is evident in the following remarks made by Congressman Underwood (1906) as he commented on the test's ability to "separate the ignorant vicious, and the lazy from the intelligent and industrious." Again, the record points to the fact that through this particular measure, officials in the United States labeled, profiled, and attempted to restrict the entrance and admittance of individuals whose race, ethnicity, or economic background prompted them to be considered undesirable.

It is clear that there were additional statutes that authorized the implementation of the quota system. This particular system emerged after the War of 1918 as Congress foresaw that the expected large immigrant influx could not be controlled by the literacy test. The quota system was based on the establishment of a preset numerical ceiling on the number of immigrants allowed to arrive in the United States during a given period.

Moreover, the strategy behind the quota system was to establish a specific numerical figure for the number of arrivals from certain countries held to be "nesting grounds" for carriers of social ills. In contrast, the nonquota classes, according to the U.S. Department of Justice (1953), included individuals who met any of the following criteria:

a.   Unmarried children under 18 years of age or wives of residents.
b.   Aliens lawfully admitted returning from a temporary visit abroad.

   c. Natives from the Western Hemisphere.

   d. Ministers of any religious denomination or any professor, his wife, and unmarried children under 18 years of age.

   e. Bona fide students.

Another statute that enabled the profiling of individuals and the selective enforcement of the law was passed on February 15, 1893. This particular statute gave the president of the United States the authority to temporarily suspend the influx of immigrants to the United States. This statute was followed by the 1952 Act, which gave the president even broader power to "suspend the entry of all aliens" whenever it was determined that their entry would be "detrimental to the interests of the United States" (U.S. Department of Justice, 1953).

Unfortunately, the labeling and profiling of individuals did not end with the enactment of immigration statutes. Rather, it was transformed to the physical isolation of individuals in immigration ports. That is, individuals who were profiled as having physical or social vulnerabilities were labeled and isolated from the rest of the immigrant population. For instance, at Ellis Island (a major immigration port), medical inspection was the first component of the screening process. It started as soon as immigrants ascended the stairs to the registry room. That is, U.S. Public Health Service doctors stationed at the top of the stairs were on careful watch for any immigrant with shortness of breath or signs of heart trouble as the new arrivals began to climb up the steps while hefting their luggage. Insofar as those stairs were concerned, immigrants would often refer to these as the "90-second physical." This name captured the essence of the mission of U.S. immigrations doctors who observed patiently to spot those deemed as unfit to enter the United States.

It was during the first face-to-face meeting with federal physicians that profiling took place in a more substantive manner. That is, physicians would screen individuals with the aim of identifying and labeling those that suffered from contagious diseases, mental abnormalities, or physical deformities, which could limit their ability to support themselves. This experience was described by immigrants as "traumatic."

It is clear that this examination process represented a preliminary attempt by immigration officials to identify those believed to pose a threat to American society. Consequently, the immigrants that were chosen (i.e., profiled) and determined to need further examination were detained and marked with chalk so that they could be identified more easily from the crowd of immigrants. Clearly, this marks another historical episode where the profiling of immigrants took place.

The marking with chalk constituted nothing more than code letters indicating the reasons for the holdover. For example, K meant the individual was suspected to have a hernia; L represented an immigrant suffering from lung complications; E meant that the new arrival could have problems related to the eyes; H signified heart-related problems; X meant that the individual was suspected of suffering from a mental disorder.

The following list originates from Kraut's book *Ellis Island: Historical Overview*, which shows some of the additional markings issued to the group of "unhealthy" immigrants at Ellis Island:

B Black
C Conjunctivitis
CT Trachoma
F Face
FT Feet
G Goiter
N Neck
L Lameness
PG Pregnancy
SC Scalp (Fungus)
S Senility

Once marked, immigrants, some of whom had received several letters, were removed from the inspection line and placed in specially designed examination rooms. In these rooms, they would be checked for further signs of illnesses.

Those whose illnesses were determined as not being severe would be sent to the hospitals for observation and care. In fact, patients who recovered and were determined not to pose a threat to society were usually allowed on land. However, others whose illnesses were incurable were deported to their countries of origin.

This traumatic experience is best described in the words of those individuals who endured it. According to Pauline Notkoff (1917), a Polish immigrant, physicians would often ask questions such as, "how much is two and one?" In her account, Notkoff stated that "the next young girl also from our city" was asked "how do you wash stairs, from the top or from the bottom?" She replied, "I don't go to America to wash stairs." Another account of this process was told in 1916 by Victoria Sarfatti Fernandez, a Macedonian Jewish immigrant. According to Fernandez, "the whole experience was very frightening . . . they brought me up to a room . . . they put a pegboard before me with little sticks of different shapes and little holes. . . . I had to put them in place, the round ones and the square ones . . . and I did it perfectly. They said 'oh, we must have made a mistake. This little girl . . . naturally she doesn't know English, but she's very bright, intelligent; they took the cross (chalkmark) off me so we were cleared."

The underlying factor that derives from this discussion is that individuals who were more likely to present illnesses originated from poor countries in Africa and other underdeveloped areas of the world. That is, people of color or those considered to be ethnically inferior were overrepresented among the isolated population at Ellis Island and other similar immigration ports. In fact, you may want to note, from the previously introduced list, that *B* (blackness) was one of several markings used to denote "abnormality." That is, one would be isolated for being black in the same manner as a person suffering from a physical disease. When reviewing the historical record, it is evident that racial profiling was also used at Ellis Island and similar reception ports during the immigration era.

CESARE LOMBROSO

Almost during the same period as the Jim Crow and immigration eras, a half world away, a physician by the name of Cesare Lombroso (1835–1909) began to identify patterns of criminality based on the physical appearances of individuals. It is said that Lombroso once said, as he performed an autopsy on an Italian convict in 1894, "At the sight of that skull, I seemed to see all of a sudden, lighted up as a vast plain under a flaming sky, the problem of the nature of the criminal." Clearly, his "scientific" method relied heavily on the observation of physical characteristics that were "unusual" in human beings. These, according to Lombroso, were indicative of criminality.

Cesare Lombroso was an Italian physician who performed numerous postmortem examinations on criminals during the late nineteenth century. According to his own reflections, he apparently noticed that many of the criminals examined shared similar physical attributes. Some of the characteristics he observed among criminals included

a. Receding hairline
b. Forehead wrinkles
c. Bumpy face
d. Broad noses
e. Fleshy lips
f. Sloping shoulders
g. Long arms
h. Pointy fingers

According to Lombroso, these characteristics were associated with those of primitive man. He called it atavism, while leaving very little doubt that its roots are found in Charles Darwin's book titled *The Origin of Species*, published in the 1870s. It was Lombroso's contention that criminals were immoral individuals who represented a throwback to primitive man. That is, criminals, according to Lombroso, had developed to the same biological level as modern (noncriminal) human beings despite the fact criminals were destined since birth to criminal behavior due, to a large extent, to their physical inferiority.

Lombroso added that the "born criminal" descended from a "degenerate family with frequent case of insanity, deafness, syphilis, epilepsy, and alcoholism among its members." As if Lombroso had not done enough to fuel the momentum to profile individuals based on their appearances, he seems to have become obsessed with the practice of tattooing. He associated the presence of tattoos to criminality, while adding that ". . . tattooing declare more than any official brief to reveal to us the fierce and obscene hearts of these unfortunates" (Lombroso, 1896). From his work on tattoos, he ended up making sweeping assumptions; in an interview, he was recorded as having stated that among the 89 tattooed people seen, "I saw seventy one who had been tattooed in prison." He added that "tattooing is, in fact, one of the essential characteristics of primitive man . . . and of men who still live in the savage state." His findings influenced others to make assumptions about individuals based on physical characteristics—clearly, a form of profiling.

WILLIAM SHELDON

Meanwhile, in the United States, an American psychologist by the name of William Sheldon (1898–1977) devoted his time to observe the range of human body types. In 1940, Sheldon studied several hundred juvenile offenders in the Boston area, while paying close attention to their bodies. While taking pictures of the juvenile offenders, Sheldon classified (i.e., profiled) body structures according to different categories. The groups were divided as follows:

a.   Mesomorphs—had a stocky and muscular build
b.   Ectomorphs—had a thin body and were typically fragile
c.   Endomorphs—described as soft, round with short limbs.

In his research, Sheldon proposed the use of a numerical scale to grade the degrees of an individual's body typology. That is, he acknowledged that people could possess varying degrees of each of the three body builds. Thus, he assigned a number from 1 through 7 in order to measure the amount of body type in each individual examined. For instance, a "pure" Mesomorph would be a 7-1-1 type. A "pure" Ectomorph would be a 1-7-1. However, a person that appeared to have traits of both body types would be a 2-6-1, and so on.

In addition to the numerical scale, Sheldon believed that each body type had a corresponding personality. That is, Endomorphs were inclined, for the most part, to physical comfort, food, and socializing, while Mesomorphs enjoyed physical action and ambition. The latter were believed to sleep the least while exhibiting a predisposition to anger. In addition, Mesomorphs were thought to be prone to gambling and were very assertive in their dealings with others. Clearly, then, Sheldon held that this body type was more closely associated to criminality than any other body type. Finally, Ectomorphs centered on privacy and restraint. They were at times described as being shy.

It is important to note that the work of Lombroso and Sheldon contributed a great deal to the beliefs held by individuals representing popular culture at the time. In other words, these "scientific" experiences transcended to the action of immigration officials in places like Ellis Island as they attempted to identify and isolate individuals of "certain" attributes. Further, I contend that the work of Lombroso and Sheldon served to promote the rationale that led to some of the injustices that took place during the Jim Crow era, as discussed earlier. The argument supporting the notion that racial profiling is a new phenomenon is simply not valid. As demonstrated in this discussion, the belief that someone is inferior to others based on that person's background is a practice that has been in existence for centuries. It is my contention that racial profiling was the tool or mechanism used in order to identify, isolate, and address (if necessary) individuals who, throughout the centuries, have been deemed as inferior or less than capable to serve as productive members of society.

THE CHICAGO SCHOOL

"The Chicago School" (an evolution-based school of thought that grew out of the economics department at the University of Chicago in the 1920s) also contributed to the spirit in which individuals were profiled based on the area in which they lived. Robert E. Park and Ernest W. Burgess conducted several research projects out of the University of Chicago, in which they elaborated on the theory of urban ecology, proposing that cities were environments like those found in nature. That is, cities were environments that were governed by the same forces that were proposed in the works of Charles Darwin. According to Park and Burgess, the most important of these forces was competition in which individuals living in depleted areas of the city of Chicago competed for the few resources available in these areas. This concept included the geographic division of the city between those that had "just arrived" as "immigrants" and those considered as productive and affluent members of the community. Needless to say, there were assumptions or underlying behavioral expectations that were provided for each "area" of the city of Chicago and its corresponding population. In my view, this constituted a form of labeling which consequently provided officials with a tool to profile given an individual's racial or ethnic background.

It is clear that since the Jim Crow and immigration eras, racial profiling has evolved throughout different historical periods. For instance, during the campaign to end drugs, law enforcement officials came up with a concept titled "drug courier profile." This, allegedly, helped them in apprehending criminals involved in the transportation and distribution of drugs.

DRUG COURIER AND SKYJACKER PROFILES

The drug courier profile was developed by Drug Enforcement Administration (DEA) agents as they sought to improve their method of intercepting and detecting drug trafficking at major airports. In fact, agent Paul Markonni is typically given credit for having created the drug courier profile for the DEA. Agent Markonni created and perfected the use of the profile while working at the Cincinnati airport; he subsequently trained fellow agents who applied it at airports throughout the United States. At one time, it was reported that the drug courier profile was in place in more than 20 airports nationwide.

The drug courier profile emanated from the creation of the skyjacker profile, which came as a result of the 1968 Federal Task Force. The Task Force was made up of representatives from different agencies, including the Department of Justice, the Federal Aeronautics Administration, the Department of Commerce, and people trained in psychology, law, and engineering. The Task Force developed a procedure based on several steps with the aim of identifying skyjackers before they boarded the plane. The idea was that as passengers passed through a metal detector, they would be observed to determine if they matched the characteristics of a hijacker profile. These characteristics were drawn from a study of previous skyjackings. The Task Force utilized statistical, sociological, and psychological data in order to come up with 25 to 30 characteristics which allowed for personnel to distinguish the traits of hijackers from the rest of the population.

It is clear, then, that the drug courier profile traces its historical origins to the skyjacker profile, as described earlier. The drug courier profile carried two different sets of characteristics. According to Heumann and Cassak (2005); these were as follows:

Primary Characteristics

    a. Arrived from or departed to an identified "source city"
    b. Little or no luggage; large numbers of empty suitcases
    c. Unusual itinerary such as a rapid turnaround time for lengthy flights
    d. Use of an alias
    e. Carrying unusually large amounts of currency (generally on the person or in a case/bag)
    f. Purchasing a ticket with a large amount of small denomination currency
    g. An unusual degree of nervousness or anxiety.

Secondary Characteristics

    a. Almost exclusive use of public transportation, particularly taxicabs, when departing from airports
    b. Immediate telephone call upon deplaning
    c. Leaving a false or fictitious number with the airline
    d. Excessively frequent travel to source or distribution cities.

Clearly, the drug courier profile had ties to the concept of racial profiling insofar as some of the characteristics listed are typical of individuals whose behavior may be depicted as "suspicious" or "unusual." This was confirmed in a testimony provided by the DEA agent Markonni, where he mentioned that "a black man arriving from a major heroin distribution point arouses greater suspicion, ceteris paribus [all things being equal] than one arriving from a major cocaine distribution point." In another case, Markonni acknowledged that most drug couriers were African American females. The testimonies provided by Markonni were supported by data supplied by his colleagues, where in one instance a police officer stated that 75% of the people stopped at the Memphis airport were African American. Further, in a survey of cases in the early 1990s it was discovered that 60 out of 63 stops involved minorities (Heumann and Cassak, 2005).

Unfortunately, these trends were not centralized in specific areas of the country; rather, this became apparent all over the United States. The DEA, believing their drug courier profile was effective, spread the word and instituted Operation Pipeline. This operation constituted an intelligence-based assessment of the method by which drug was transported to different markets. It also included interaction with highway drug enforcement techniques. Under this particular operation, police officers were trained to apply a profile that included evidence of concealment in the vehicle, fast driving, and age and race characteristics of the likely offensive drivers. In some cases, the profiling techniques were distorted in order for officers to target black and Hispanic male drivers while stopping them with the pretext of having committed technical traffic violations.

NEW JERSEY HIGHWAYS

The selective targeting of highway drivers continued throughout the years and became apparent in cases involving New Jersey state troopers. In several instances, New Jersey troopers were involved in activities with minority drivers that seemed to fall outside the scope of a typical routine traffic stop. In fact, the case that brought national attention to the topic of racial profiling involved two New Jersey state troopers who fired 11 shots into a van carrying four black men on their way to a basketball clinic. After the shooting, the troopers brought in drug-sniffing dogs in an attempt to find drugs in order to make it seem that the shooting had been justified. To the displeasure of the troopers, they found only basketball equipment and a bible.

In addition to facing criminal charges, the troopers also faced charges for falsely claiming that they thought the men involved in this incident were white. As part of the plea agreement that ultimately resolved the case, the troopers were allowed to plead guilty to reduced charges while being spared both jail time and probation. As he approved the plea bargain, Judge Charles A. Delehey of the State Superior Court in Mercer County told the troopers that "you are the victims not only of your own actions, but of the system, which employed you." In other words, the judge acknowledged that the troopers were carrying out policies that they had been instructed to.

This particular plea agreement came on the heels of the decision made by the U.S. District Court judge Joel Pisano to allow the four minority victims to move forward with claims that the state violated their constitutional rights through racial profiling, and that top state officials including former New Jersey attorney general Peter Verniero and former superintendents of state police Clinton Pagano and Carl Williams acted with deliberate indifference rather than attempting to stop the practice. It should be noted that Superintendent Williams once told a local newspaper (*Newark Star-Ledger*), when responding to recently released data suggesting that 75% of all motorists arrested on the New Jersey Turnpike in the first two months of 1997 were minorities, that cocaine and marijuana traffickers were more likely to be either black or Hispanic. These comments gave rise to a public outcry that resulted in his termination by New Jersey governor Christine Todd Whitman.

Other incidents involving professionals who commuted through the New Jersey highways also resulted in litigation and publicity nationwide. One of these cases involved a black dentist from East Orange, New Jersey. According to reports, the dentist drove a BMW and was stopped for motor vehicle violations on the New Jersey Turnpike approximately one hundred times between 1984 and 1988. During some of the stops, police officers asked to search his trunk; in one of these stops he refused, so the trooper took his license and registration back to the police car, forcing the dentist to wait 15 to 20 minutes before returning these documents to him. The dentist learned, he affirmed later on, that it was better to consent to the search than risk being late for his patients (Heumann and Cassak, 2005).

These cases gave rise to a national awareness regarding the practice of racial profiling. In fact, the response was overwhelming, with civil rights organizations aligning themselves to offer a strong voice against this particular practice. Lawsuits were filed in almost every instance where a case involving an apparent racial profiling incident was detected.

DRIVING WHILE BLACK

Perhaps the most notorious response by civil rights groups to the apparent growing trend of racial profiling incidents in the United States, was the publication titled *Driving While Black: Racial Profiling on Our Nation's Highways*. This document, published in 1999, was drafted by attorney David Harris, University of Toledo College of Law, under the direction of the American Civil Liberties Union (ACLU). It was Mr. Harris's publication that gave rise to a much-heated debate at the national level regarding racial profiling. *Driving While Black* was filled with anecdotes from individuals recounting their profiling experiences. The first page of the report contained the following story:

> On a hot summer afternoon in August 1998, 37-year-old U.S. Army Sergeant First Class Rossano V. Gerald and his young son Gregory drove across the Oklahoma border into a nightmare. A career soldier and a highly decorated veteran of Desert Storm and Operation United Shield in Somalia, SFC Gerald, a black man of Panamanian descent, found that he could not travel more than 30 minutes through the state without being stopped twice: first by the Roland City Police Department, and then by the Oklahoma Highway Patrol.
>
> During the second stop, which lasted two-and-half hours, the troopers terrorized SFC Gerald's 12-year-old son with a police dog, placed both father and son in a closed car with the air conditioning off and fans blowing hot air, and warned that the dog would attack if they attempted to escape. Halfway through the episode—perhaps realizing the extent of their lawlessness—the troopers shut off the patrol car's video evidence camera.

Given the graphic descriptions of anecdotes from individuals subject to racial profiling, the ACLU report *Driving While Black* received national attention that brought policymakers together to discuss ways in which racial profiling could be banned. In fact, the national debate was elevated to the level of the U.S. presidency when the Clinton White House, at the heels of the release of the ACLU report, invited legislators, academics, civil libertarians, and practitioners to participate in the "Strengthening Community Partnerships" conference (held in Washington, DC, in June, 1999). At this conference, the issue of racial profiling was debated from almost all perspectives. The debate resulted in several mandates from the federal government to ensure that none of its law enforcement representatives were engaging in this practice. Clinton opened the conference by stating that "As a society, we do not have to choose between keeping people safe and treating them right, between enforcing the law and upholding civil rights. We can do both." In addition, Clinton stated that we should think of racial profiling as a "morally indefensive and deeply corrosive" practice (Clinton, 1999).

At the end of the conference, President Clinton directed the Departments of Justice, Treasury, and Agriculture to also collect data on the race, ethnicity, and gender of all individuals subject to stops by federal law enforcement officials. Further, after one year, these entities were to report on the findings of the new data collection system and make recommendations based on those findings. In addition, President Clinton expressed his support for legislation for states and local law enforcement agencies to collect similar data. The rationale was that in addition to a federal commitment to ban racial profiling, the collection and analysis of data would somehow reveal internal practices relevant to racial profiling. This, coupled with the presidential support to increase resources for police integrity and ethics training (20 million dollars), was viewed as a successful tactic to help improve civil rights practices in the United States. The training was only one of several components of the Presidential Crime Bill, which specifically provided for an increase in funds for police scholarships, minority recruitment efforts, video cameras in police vehicles, and citizen police academies.

Perhaps no other public official was as vocal on racial profiling, at the time, than former U.S. attorney general Janet Reno. At the Strengthening Community Partnerships conference, Reno added that "We must leave here . . . with a commitment to put into place concrete steps that will reduce the potential for instances of excessive force and racial profiling and that will strengthen relations between the police and the community." In addition, she added that "When citizens do not trust their local police officer they are less willing to report crime (and) less willing to be witnesses to criminal cases . . . jurors are less willing to accept as truthful the testimony of officers; and recruitment of police officers from minority communities becomes that much more difficult." Clearly, Attorney General Reno's remarks found an echo across the United States as states began to adopt legislation, following the lead from the federal government, to ban racial profiling practices.

At the state level, it is reported that approximately half of the states in the United States have enacted or are in the process of enacting legislation relevant to racial profiling. These demographics will be discussed in detail later on in this book. For now, it is important to note that states continue to consider the enactment of racial profiling legislation which requires the collection and analysis of data related to traffic stops in an attempt to provide transparency in law enforcement activities before the community at large.

The review of some of the historical eras in which individuals, for one reason or another, labeled and subsequently profiled others gives us a clear sense that racial profiling, as we know it today, is a practice that dates back to early periods of American history. The practice is not new but it has recently taken a different form. That is, it could be argued that it is a practice not necessarily announced or visible (in some cases); thus, there is a sense that racial profiling occurs behind the scenes, ultimately misleading or, in some cases, misinforming members of a community about police practices and behaviors.

I want to be clear on the fact that this statement is in no way a condemnation of all police practices, as in the course of many years of working closely with law enforcement I have come to realize that there are good and honest individuals who proudly serve and protect their communities in their capacity as law enforcement professionals. Sadly, at times, their good work goes unnoticed and it is often offset by incidents where unethical and unprofessional behavior takes place. In some instances, the racially motivated unethical behavior of law enforcement personnel results in loss of life. Perhaps, one of the most significant impacts of racial profiling on members of the community relates to the notion that some members of the minority community are currently experiencing an ever-increasing lack of satisfaction in police services and a lack of confidence in the ability of officers to perform their tasks.

The apparent lack of trust and deep conviction that governs the belief that a person is stopped because of their race and not due to a traffic violation dates back to the historical eras in which African Americans and other minority members of the community were mistreated. Further, it is perpetuated generation-to-generation as many minorities are taught early in childhood how to "survive" an encounter with law enforcement officers. This approach, which appears to be "defensive" in nature, dates back to the lack of trust minorities held toward law enforcement or anyone in a position of authority in the early stages of American history.

The degree to which members of minority groups don't trust those in authority has become clearer because of recent protests, such as those launched by civil rights activist Reverend Jesse Jackson, to bring attention to what some have labeled as "delayed federal assistance" to people awaiting rescue in New Orleans during Hurricane Katrina. The point made by Reverend Jackson is that the delayed assistance took place because there was an apparent disregard for the victims due to the fact that most of those waiting to be rescued were African Americans. Jackson (2005) stated that "delays in calling for an evacuation of New Orleans virtually guaranteed that the lives threatened in the aftermath of the hurricane would be the oldest, poorest, youngest and the blackest."

Regardless of how you may feel about the remarks made by Reverend Jackson, it is clear that the racial divide in the United States is alive and well. Further, it is also clear that we will continue to have differences of opinion as to why one group may appear to be treated differently from another. It is my sincere hope that this book will contribute to the process of uncovering the underlying principles governing the racial divide in the United States. Perhaps one day we can all sit down at the same table to begin a sincere and long-awaited dialogue that will make us a "nation of one color and race."

References

Abbott, Edith (1969). *Historical Aspects of the Immigration Problem*. Chicago, IL: The University of Chicago Press.

Clinton, William J. (1999). *Comments made at the Strengthening Community Partnerships Conference*. Washington, DC. Reported by CNN, June 9, 1999.

Darwin, Charles (1859). *The Origin of Species*. London: J. Murray.

Davis, Ronald J. (2005). *From Terror to Triumph: Historical Overview*. http://www.jimcrowhistory.org/history/overview.htm

Fernandez, Victoria S. (1916). Interview conducted in 1985. Found in http://www.powayusd.com/online/usonline/worddoc/ellisislandsite.htm

Harris, David A. (1999). *Driving While Black: Racial Profiling on Our Nation's Highways*. American Civil Liberties Union Special Report.

Heumann, Milton and Cassak, Lance (2005). *Good Cop, Bad Cop: Racial Profiling and Competing Views of Justice*. Peter Lang: New York.

Hutchinson, E.P. (1981). *Legislative History of American Immigration Policy (1798–1965)*. Philadelphia, PA: University of Pennsylvania Press.

Jackson, Jesse (2005). "Jackson Says Sluggish Response Threatened Poorest and Blackest." *Shreveport Times*, September 5, 2005.

Kraut, Alan H. (1955). *Ellis Island: Historical Overview*. University Publications of America.

Lodge, Henry C. (1891). *The Restrictions of Immigration*. North American Review. January, 1891.

Lombroso, Cesare (1894, 1896). *The Born Criminal*. Court TV's Crime Library. http://www.crimelibrary.com/criminal_mind/psychology/crime_motivation/4.html?sect=19

Notkoff, Pauline (1917). Interview. Ellis Island Archives. New York, NY.

Park, Robert E. and Burgess, W. Ernest (1952). *The City and Human Ecology*. Glencoe, IL: Free Press.

Reno, Janet (1999). *Comments made at the Strengthening Community Partnerships Conference*. Washington, DC. Reported by CNN, June 9, 1999.

Sheldon, William (1940). *Somatotypes*. Cited in Phares, J.E. (1991). *Introduction to Personality* (3rd ed.). New York: Harper Collins.

Underwood, A. (1906). *Congressional Record* 40 (June 25, 1906): 9155.

U.S. Department of Justice, Immigration and Naturalization Service (1953). *Laws Applicable to Immigration and Nationality*. Washington, DC: U.S. Government Printing Office.

CHAPTER 2

The Bureau of Justice Statistics Study

Several state-based studies have attempted to capture the "true picture" of racial profiling trends in different areas of the United States. These studies have been commissioned for the most part by local authorities or advocacy groups attempting to highlight these trends. However, at the federal level, only a few studies have been produced by the U.S. Department of Justice in an attempt to comply with the presidential directive issued by former president Bill Clinton to collect and analyze racial profiling data.

The hope of federal authorities participating in the study of racial profiling has also been to set the tone for some states to follow, particularly those that have not participated in statewide racial profiling studies. While some states have followed the initiative established by the federal government to collect and analyze data, others have simply not accepted the notion that racial profiling should be identified, addressed, and consequently abolished.

The underlying factor governing the "type" of data collected and analyzed is based on the reasoning that racial profiling is believed to take place, for the most part, during the course of traffic-related contacts. This is an important point to note as the proceeding discussion will focus on data collected by the federal government that relates, for the most part, to traffic-related contacts only. Although I do not refute the fact that most racial profiling activity may take place in traffic-related incidents, it should be noted that based on this fact some states enacted laws that were designed to capture exclusively traffic-related contacts. Thus, these states have disregarded contacts made by law enforcement officers with members of the community at large in settings other than traffic-related ones, such as when they conduct a criminal investigation or serve a warrant, or during pedestrian contacts or incidents involving calls for service. This limits the ability of researchers to perform competent analysis in an attempt to determine racial profiling trends.

THE BJS CONTROVERSY

Although numerous studies on racial profiling have been conducted, none have been given more credibility or acceptance than a recently released study by the Bureau of Justice Statistics (BJS). The study *Contacts between Police and the Public* (2005) was authored, on behalf of BJS, by Matthew R. Durose, Erica L. Schmitt, and Patrick A. Langan. It is due to the great magnitude and scope of the study that it is imperative that the central areas of the study and its findings are discussed in this chapter. Thus, the following discussion will focus, for the most part, on the findings produced in this study.

As if racial profiling is not controversial enough, the release of the BJS study has encountered an unusual amount of controversy. For example, according to the *New York Times* (August 24, 2005), the director of the BJS, Lawrence A. Greenfeld, was replaced after 23 years of service. Accordingly, Mr. Greenfeld, originally named by President Bush in 2001 to lead BJS, was asked to leave and transfer to another agency after allegedly complaining to senior political officials that BJS statisticians had been asked, by government officials, to play down the racial profiling data findings to be presented in the study. Despite Mr. Greenfeld's transfer, the study was released and it is not presently known if the released version has been modified, and to what extent, from its original draft. Nevertheless, the BJS study findings reveal, for the first time, national trends with respect to police treatment of minority drivers. It is clear, then, that this report deserves much attention and as such will serve as the basis for discussion in this chapter.

Contacts between Police and the Public (2005), hereafter "the study," was based on data relevant to traffic-related contacts that took place in 2002. Before discussing the findings produced in this particular study, it is important to understand that law enforcement regards traffic contacts as opportunities to interact with the public. Some police departments who have adopted community policing initiatives feel that traffic-related contacts provide them the opportunity to identify and respond, if necessary, to incidents that relate to criminality. In other words, they rely on the notion that traffic stops provide the opportunity to detect criminal elements in the community. That is, the traffic-related circumstance or violation that may have aroused the attention of the officer to initiate the traffic stop in the first place may lead to contraband being seized or an arrest being made.

FACE-TO-FACE CONTACTS

The findings presented in the study suggest that in 2002, an estimated 45.3 million individuals (21% of the 216 million U.S. residents age 16 or older) had at least one face-to-face contact with a law enforcement officer. In addition, the findings provide insights into the nature and other demographical features of these contacts. For example, most of the citizens who have made contacts with police officers and are Caucasian males who were, at the time of contact, between 20 and 24 years old. You can refer to Table 2–1 to become acquainted with the specific figures relevant to the demographics of contacts made in 2002.

Table 2–1   Face-to-Face Contacts between Police and Citizens (2002)

Demographic Characteristic	Contact with Police	Rate of Contact per 1,000 Persons
Gender		
Male	23,884,649	230
Female	21,394,234	192
Race/Hispanic origin		
White	34,743,452	221
Black	4,966,388	193
Hispanic	4,191,712	175
Other race	1,377,332	162
Age		
16–17	1,720,202	208
18–19	2,594,029	324
20–24	6,074,822	313
25–29	4,842,871	273
30–34	4,573,911	234
35–39	5,171,387	245
40–44	5,024,133	218
45–49	4,470,583	212
50 or older	10,806,946	140
Size of jurisdiction where resided		
Under 100,000	34,580,825	212
100,000–499,999	6,763,356	226
500,000–999,999	1,818,598	228
1 million or more	2,116,106	149
Total	45,278,884	210

Source: Contacts between Police and the Public (2005). Bureau of Justice Statistics

As suggested in Table 2–1, most contacts took place with males. In fact, males had a per capita rate of contact of about 20% higher than their female counterparts. Of the male resident population, about 1 out of every 4.3 age 16 or older had a contact with a police officer. However, among females these figures were different: There was 1 contact for every 5.2 female residents age 16 or older.

Table 2–1 also shows that the rates of contacts between residents and the police varied depending on race and ethnicity. It clearly shows that whites experienced the most contact with law enforcement officers: 1 person for every 4.5 non-Hispanic white residents age 16 or older. Accordingly, about 1 person for every 5.2 black residents and, at a lower rate, about 1 Hispanic for every 5.7 persons of Hispanic origin had a direct contact with a police officer. When considering per capita data, the rate of police–resident contact for whites was approximately 15% higher than that for blacks and about 26% higher than that for Hispanics. It is clear, after reviewing the data, that other races (i.e., Asians, Pacific Islanders, American Indians, and Alaska Natives) experienced contacts with law enforcement officers at lower rates than whites and blacks. That is, there was an average contact rate of 1 person for every 6.2 residents of other races.

As expected, younger residents had more frequent contact with the police when compared to their older counterparts. Accordingly, residents in the age groups of 18–19 and 20–24 had the highest rates of police contacts (approximately 1 for every 3.1 persons and about 1 for every 3.2 persons, respectively). Unlike young residents, individuals who were 50 or older experienced a rate of contact of 1 for every 7.1 persons of this age group.

Size of Jurisdiction

Individuals who lived in jurisdictions with fewer than 100,000 residents experienced a rate of contact with police that was 42% higher than that for those who resided in jurisdictions of 1 million or more residents. Restated, this constitutes 212 instead of 149 per 1,000 residents.

REASONS FOR TRAFFIC STOPS

The underlying notion of traffic-related racial profiling is that minority motorists are being stopped for reasons other than traffic-related violations. Thus, it is imperative that we explore the results of the *Contacts between Police and the Public* (2005) study in light of the "reasons" given for police contacts (see Table 2–2).

As illustrated in Table 2–2, most of the contacts with citizens were police initiated. The remaining contacts (41.5%) were initiated by someone other than police officers, including, but not exclusively, family members or acquaintances of family members.

Of the reasons for contact, most contacts (17 million) took place when a driver was pulled over by a police officer. This is consistent with the rationale used by legislators considering the enactment of racial profiling legislation prompting the collection and analysis of traffic-related data specifically targeting contacts made with the police as a citizen is pulled over. The remaining traffic-related contacts (1.2 million) took place in instances where an individual was a passenger in a vehicle that was pulled over by a police officer. It is equally important to note that, according to the study, the second frequent reason for face-to-face contacts with police was to report a crime or problem: Among the 45.3 million people that experienced police contacts, approximately 1 in 4 contacted police because of these reasons.

Reason and Disposition of Contact

In the racial profiling debate, it is often argued that after the contact is made with the citizen, police at times resort to practices that "reveal" their true biased intentions of engaging

Table 2–2   Reasons for Traffic-Related Contacts

	Contacts with Police	
	Number	**Percentage**
Type of contact		
Police-initiated	26,483,794	58.5
Not police-initiated*	18,795,090	41.5
Reason for contact		
Traffic accident	5,891,645	13.0
Driver during traffic stop	16,783,467	37.1
Passenger during traffic stop	1,218,470	2.7
Reported crime or problem to police	11,959,548	26.4
Police provided assistance or service	3,264,503	7.2
Police were investigating crime	2,615,255	5.8
Suspected of something by police	1,158,167	2.6
Other reason	2,387,828	5.3
Total	45,278,884	100

Source: Contacts between Police and the Public (2005). Bureau of Justice Statistics
*Includes contact initiated by the resident or someone other than the police (i.e., family member or acquaintance of resident).

in racial profiling practices. That is, supporters of this notion argue that after the police make the initial stop, they simply don't discover any contraband or find a reason to arrest the citizen. Thus, according to them, traffic-related contact data, once collected and analyzed, shows a weak "productivity" record. That is, the data seems to suggest, by virtue of the absence of contraband found or arrest being made, that the stop was simply not based on legitimate traffic-related violations. In this context, it is important to review the reason for contact and arrest data reported in the study (see Table 2–3).

Police practices dictate that when an arrest takes place, police don't always handcuff the suspect. Further, not all persons who are handcuffed are subsequently arrested. In fact, in some cases, handcuffs are used to restrain the suspect while the initial assessment on how to handle a situation takes place. According to the study, in 2002, approximately 1.3 million residents age 16 or older were arrested. This constituted about 2.9% of the 45.3 million persons who came in contact with the police (see Table 2–3). In addition, approximately 1.3 million residents were reportedly handcuffed during their contact with the police.

Approximately 4.3% of residents were placed under arrest. However, in the case of non–police-initiated contacts, less than 1% were arrested. That is, if an individual initiated

Table 2–3   Type of Reason and Disposition of Police Contacts

	Characteristics of Police Contact		
	Handcuffed the Resident (%)	Arrested the Resident (%)	Resident Feels Officer(s) Acted Properly (%)
Type of contact			
Police-initiated	4.3	4.3	87.6
Not police-initiated*	0.9	0.8	93.6
Reason for contact			
Traffic accident	2.0	2.0	93.1
Driver during traffic stop	2.8	2.7	89.3
Passenger during traffic stop	5.8	5.5	80.6
Reported crime or problem to police	0.6	0.6	93.0
Police provided assistance or service	0.6	0.3	96.1
Police were investigating crime	8.3	8.2	86.7
Suspected of something by police	21.3	22.1	68.9
Other reason	4.2	5.1	83.6
Estimated number	1,301,987	1,302,417	40,790,830
Total	2.9	2.9	90.1

Source: *Contacts between Police and the Public* (2005). Bureau of Justice Statistics
*Includes contact initiated by the resident or someone other than the police (i.e., family member or acquaintance of resident).

the contact with the police they were not likely to be subject to an arrest. Again, this corresponds with the commonly held belief that most arrests take place when the police initiate contact with an individual.

With regard to the opinion given by residents with respect to police contacts, the findings suggested that in 2002, the majority (90.1%) of individuals felt the police acted properly. However, people whose contact was not initiated by the police (93.6%) were more likely than those whose contact was police initiated (87.6%) to feel officers acted properly in the course of their encounter. This makes sense as typically people who may call for police help are more likely to have confidence in the police in the first place.

Legitimacy of Stop

When controlling for race and ethnicity, the findings suggested minor differences among gender and racial/ethnic groups with regard to their opinion on whether or not the police had legitimate reasons to stop them (see Table 2–4). Females (86%) were more likely than males (82%) to feel they had been stopped for legitimate reasons. With regard to race, the majority of blacks (73%) felt that they were stopped for legitimate reasons. However, blacks were less likely than their white (86%) counterparts and somewhat less likely than Hispanics (82%) to say that they had been stopped for legitimate reasons.

It should be noted that age did not seem to be a factor when being asked if the stop was legitimate. That is, individuals from all age groups represented in this particular study seem to agree that the reason why they had been stopped was legitimate. In other words, they felt they deserved to be stopped.

You should pause a bit and reflect on these figures as they highlight important factors underlying the racial profiling issue. For instance, some people erroneously believe that most members of minority groups contend that the police stop them due to illegitimate reasons. Clearly, the findings introduced in this study counter this position, as it is evident

Table 2–4   Opinions on Legitimacy of Stop while Controlling for Race and Ethnicity

	Percentage of Stopped Drivers who Felt that They Had Been Stopped for a Legitimate Reason
Gender	
Male	82
Female	86
Race/Hispanic origin	
White	86
Black	73
Hispanic	82
Other race	83
Age	
16–19	84
20–29	83
30–39	85
40–49	84
50–59	85
60 or older	83
Total	84

Source: Contacts between Police and the Public (2005). Bureau of Justice Statistics

that most minority members agree that the stop made was legitimate. However, we should appreciate the fact that minorities in general and blacks in particular are less willing to accept the notion that they had been stopped for legitimate reasons when compared to their white counterparts. The underlying reason for this will be discussed in later chapters.

Time of Stop

Another interesting variable to consider is the time in which drivers were stopped. That is, if we were to agree with the notion, for argument sake, that most police officers stop blacks since they are able to identify the race of the driver, then we should accept that daytime as opposed to nighttime conditions are more suitable for this practice. That is, if in fact racial profiling is taking place in police-related contacts, then the data should suggest a greater percentage of blacks being stopped during daytime hours, when compared to the percentage of blacks being stopped at night. In order to investigate this issue, researchers of the study compared the daytime and nighttime traffic stops for whites and blacks. As is evident from Table 2–5 a smaller percentage of blacks were stopped in the daytime hours than at nighttime. That is, of the 4.6 million white and black drivers stopped at night, about 700,000 (15%) were black. These findings suggest that blacks constituted a smaller and not a greater percentage of daytime (11%) than nighttime (15%) traffic stops. This, therefore, shows that visibility of the driver did not seem to be a factor when comparing daytime versus nighttime driving populations. However, a word of caution is in order: Despite the belief that some of you may adopt—after reviewing the data discussed earlier which allegedly supports the notion that police officers don't specifically attempt to identify the race of the driver in daytime traffic contacts—the possibility that some police officers may engage in racial profiling in a nonconventional manner cannot be discarded. That is, some police officers may target neighborhoods, during both day and night, where blacks seem to be well represented. Further, it could also be that some police officers may be more inclined to stop vehicles at night that may appear to be driven by blacks or perhaps to engage in selective enforcement practices in black neighborhoods. Although the data produced here does not necessarily support or counter these possibilities, we are

Table 2–5   Time of Day of Traffic Stop

Race of Driver Stopped	Drivers Stopped			
	During the Day		At Night	
	Number	Percentage	Number	Percentage
White	9,000,000	89	3,900,000	85
Black	1,100,000	11	700,000	15
Total	10,100,000	100	4,600,000	100

Source: Contacts between Police and the Public (2005). Bureau of Justice Statistics

obliged to continue keeping an open mind when considering these and other factors that may influence police-related behavior regarding minority contacts during daytime and nighttime conditions.

SEARCH PATTERNS

Some scholars and civil rights advocates regard racial profiling not only as the act of stopping someone based on their race and ethnicity but also as the taking of unjustified action once the individual has been stopped—that is, searching a person or vehicle due largely to the color of the skin or ethnicity of the individual (which is unlawful) as opposed to the 24 suspicion that criminal activity may have taken place (which warrants a lawful search). In the study, the researchers found that among motorists stopped by police officers, blacks (10.2%) and Hispanics (11.4%) were more likely than whites (3.5%) to be physically searched or to have their vehicle searched. Further, it was found that police officers were more likely to search a vehicle driven by either a black (7.1%) or Hispanic (10.1%) than by a white (2.9%).

When considering search data, we should pause and reflect on the exact meaning/value of this particular source of information. That is, search data largely reflects the initiative of a police officer to search a vehicle or a person; this action is based on suspicion that contraband may be found. The rationale is that by seeking more evidence, the police officer will be able to formulate a full assessment of the situation. Although it could be argued that by analyzing the end result of a search (i.e., whether or not contraband was found), one can appreciate a better picture of whether or not the search was justified, the truth of the matter is that the nature of police searches is complex and deserves some attention.

Searches are not necessarily racist in nature if they don't produce contraband. However, in specific cases, one can review the record of a particular police officer and understand a bit more comprehensively whether that officer has racial tendencies when performing searches. That is, if the officer seems to search mostly minorities and if these particular searches seldom produce contraband, this may likely raise red flags to police administrators that there may be behavioral issues to correct in this individual. On the other hand, if a police officer is assigned to a predominately minority area of town, how can he or she escape the unavoidable fact that the searches he or she is likely to perform will, for the most part, involve minorities?

Perhaps the strongest argument to consider when debating the value of search data pertains to the notion that researchers are unable to predict if a particular search was warranted. That is, did the individual being searched deserve to be under some degree of scrutiny by the law enforcement officer, ultimately resulting in a search? The answer to this question is hardly revealed when analyzing statistical data relevant to police searches. In other words, it always comes back to the individual officer. That is, was the officer searching a suspect due to that individual's race or ethnicity or would the officer have performed a search despite the individual's racial/ethnic makeup?

OUTCOME OF SEARCHES

While keeping these points in mind, we should also focus on the findings produced in the study with respect to the type and outcome of searches while controlling for race/ethnicity (see Table 2–6).

The data presented in Table 2–6 suggests that the majority of males and females gave consent to police officers to search their vehicle/person. However, when considering race/ethnicity, the findings differed, in some cases, among the different racial/ethnic groups measured. According to the data, the majority of white and Hispanic drivers gave consent when asked if they could be searched. However, among blacks, the

Table 2–6   Type and Outcome of Searches Conducted by Police during Traffic Stops (2002)

Demographic Characteris- tics of Searched Driver	Search of the Driver or the Vehicle				
	Type of Search			Outcome of Search	
	All Searches (%)	With Consent (%)	Without Consent (%)	Evidence Found (%)	No Evidence Found (%)
Gender					
Male	100	53.6	46.4	10.5	89.5
Female	100	61.4	38.6	19.2*	80.8
Race/Hispanic origin					
White	100	60.9	39.1	14.5	85.5
Black	100	41.4	58.6	3.3*	96.7
Hispanic	100	53.8	46.2	13.0	87.0
Other race	100	51.9*	48.1*	26.5*	73.5*
Age					
16–19	100	49.4	50.6	21.6*	78.4
20–29	100	60.2	39.8	11.6*	88.4
30–39	100	58.0	42.0	7.8*	92.2
40–49	100	47.6	52.4	4.6*	95.4
50–59	100	24.7*	75.3*	21.7*	78.3*
60 or older	—	—	—	—	—
Estimated number	837,809	458,338	379,471	98,394	739,415
Total	100	54.7	45.3	11.7	88.3

Source: Contacts between Police and the Public (2005). Bureau of Justice Statistics
*Estimate is based on ten or fewer sample cases.

majority of drivers did not give police officers consent for searches. When considering age groups, most consented to searches except for those in age groups of 16–19, 40–49, and 50–59.

When reviewing data relevant to the outcome of the search, it is clear that criminal evidence was not found in most searches. However, there were some noticeable differences among races/ethnicities. That is, criminal evidence was more likely to have been found among whites (14.5%) than blacks (3.3%) or Hispanics (13.0%). This constitutes a major finding in that despite the fact the majority of black drivers did not consent to be searched, a very small percentage of these searches resulted in the detection of criminal evidence. In contrast, the majority of white drivers consented to be searched and a greater percentage of these searches (when compared to blacks and Hispanics) resulted in criminal evidence being identified and seized. Some may argue, when reviewing these figures, that since most black and Hispanic searches (despite their large volume) have not resulted in the discovery of criminal evidence, drivers from these particular minority groups may be subject of unnecessary and unjustified searches.

None of us can easily discard the possibility that, in fact, these figures suggest a bias on the part of law enforcement officials. That is, there is a possibility that some law enforcement officers, when interacting with minority drivers, become suspicious of their activities (due entirely to the race of the driver), which ultimately leads to officers performing a high volume of searches that don't produce criminal evidence. However, there are also other possibilities that should be explored. For example, it could be that officers in predominately minority/poor neighborhoods become more suspicious of minority/poor drivers due to the fact that more crime is reported in these areas, thus, leading to a psychology of suspicion on all contacts. Further, the absence of a high volume of searches resulting in the discovery of criminal evidence could be explained in terms of routine investigatory activity on behalf of the officer. For example, there are legal circumstances that require officers to perform searches (i.e., inventory searches) when individuals are arrested. These non-discretionary searches don't necessarily require the officer to determine prior to the search if the individual is suspicious of possessing contraband. Rather, these searches are mandatory and they rest on the legal premise that the vehicle seized/towed at the time of arrest will be returned (by virtue of the information recorded in the inventory) to the owner in the same manner and with the same equipment as found at the time it was towed. Typically, these inventory searches do not reveal criminal evidence that may be utilized against the individual already taken into custody. Thus, the failure in distinguishing these inventory searches from other searches may lead individuals to erroneously conclude that most searches don't produce evidence and therefore are to some extent unjustified. In fact, the figures obtained and analyzed in the study suggest that of the nearly 450,000 drivers arrested during a traffic stop in 2002, approximately 3 quarters (74%) or slightly more than 329,000 drivers were also searched (vehicle or person, or both). It is reported that an estimated 26% of the 329,000 searches were physical searches of the driver, 9% were vehicle searches, and 65% of drivers experienced both a physical and vehicle search.

USE OF FORCE

The study produced additional findings with regard to the use of force against drivers generally and minorities specifically, in the course of a traffic-related contact (see Table 2–7).

The data suggests that with respect to gender, a greater percentage of males, when compared to females, who came in contact with the police were subject to use of force. In addition, among all races/ethnicities that came in contact with the police, a greater percentage of blacks (3.5%), when compared to all other races/ethnicities, were either threatened or subject to use of force by police. The second largest percentage in this category related to Hispanic contacts (2.5%). In other words, whites that came in contact

Table 2–7   Contacts and Police Use of Force Demographics

Demographic Characteristic	Number of Persons with Police Contact	Contacts with Police in Which Force was Used or Threatened	
		Number	**Percentage**
Gender			
Male	23,884,649	520,178	2.2
Female	21,394,234	144,281	0.7
Race/Hispanic origin			
White	34,743,452	373,847	1.1
Black	4,966,388	172,658	3.5
Hispanic	4,191,712	102,670	2.5
Other race	1,377,332	15,284	1.1*
Age			
16–19	4,314,231	152,118	3.5
20–29	10,917,693	230,028	2.1
30–39	9,745,298	116,774	1.2
40–49	9,494,716	95,285	1.0
50–59	6,006,828	49,717	0.8
60 or older	4,800,117	20,537	0.4*
Size of jurisdiction where resided			
Under 100,000	34,580,825	434,142	1.3
100,000–499,999	6,763,356	112,213	1.7
500,000–999,999	1,818,598	54,489	3.0
1 million or more	2,116,106	63,614	3.0
Total	45,278,884	664,458	1.5

Source: Contacts between Police and the Public (2005). Bureau of Justice Statistics

*Estimate is based on ten or fewer sample cases.

with the police were the least subject to threats or use of force. This finding is interesting in light of the earlier data discussed (Table 2–6) with regard to the criminal evidence produced. That is, despite the fact black searches did not produce, for the most part, criminal evidence, blacks were still subject to a greater degree, than any other race, to the use of force by police. This could be explained one of two ways—blacks give police greater reason than any other racial group to use force or perhaps law enforcement officials are more likely to use force when interacting with blacks due to reasons related to racism. Unfortunately, the available data is inconclusive in this regard as it fails to provide "reasons" why this particular phenomenon takes place. However, researchers should explore the benefits associated with qualitative analysis on this topic; this perhaps may result in the identification and analysis of the "reasons" cited by police officers that somehow justified the threat or use of force. It should also be noted that the data on use of force also highlighted the fact that 16- to 19-year-olds were exposed to the most threats or use of force incidents, among all age groups. In addition, most threats or use of force incidents took place in jurisdictions of under 100,000 residents.

Injuries Due to Use of Force

When considering the percentage of individuals who were injured in use of force incidents, there were also noticeable differences detected among racial/ethnic groups (see Table 2–8).

As is evident in this particular table, Hispanics constituted the racial/ethnic group with the most significant percentage of drivers that were injured during traffic-related contacts. This was followed by blacks and whites, in that order. Thus, in addition to the fact that minority contacts produced the least percentage of criminal evidence while experiencing the most significant percentage of incidents related to threats or use of force, it should be noted that among those use of force incidents, minorities, once again, experienced the most injuries.

Table 2–8   Police Use of Force and Injuries

Race/Hispanic Origin of Resident	Number of Persons Threatened or against Whom Force Was Used	Persons Injured during Contact in which Force Was Used	
		Number	Percentage
White	373,847	43,637	11.7
Black	172,658	26,530	15.4*
Hispanic	102,670	22,101	21.5*
Other race	15,284	0	0*
Total	664,458	92,268	13.9

Source: Contacts between Police and the Public (2005). Bureau of Justice Statistics
*Estimate is based on ten or fewer sample cases.

INTERPRETING THE DATA

Although I would caution the reader against interpreting these findings conclusively one way or another, they should be considered as early indicators of contact-related patterns nationwide. It becomes clear, after reviewing the contact data produced in the BJS study, that although most contacts don't produce criminal evidence, searches take place at a higher percentage among minorities. Further, it is also clear that minorities are also more likely to experience threats or use of force incidents that ultimately may result in injuries to them. Why is this the case, you may wonder? Although we have covered in this chapter a few explanations that may qualify as logical and balanced, when addressing the data findings, it is important to consider the fact that statistics don't typically lie; however, statisticians do!

I am also sure you have realized by now that the "meaning" of the data depends on your perspective or the ideology you follow. If you are an individual who believes that most law enforcement personnel are biased and that they engage in traffic-related contacts with minorities to harass or intimidate them, perhaps you will also hold true the notion that the biased nature of policing explains why minorities are disproportionately searched and subjected to use of force incidents. However, if you follow the ideology that police officers, for the most part, are good and honest people, perhaps you may be inclined to believe that the data shown in the BJS study is incomplete and fails to provide "reasons" as to why minorities seem to be searched more frequently or are subject to use of force incidents. It all depends on your perspective.

In case the uncertainty frustrates your ongoing quest to find out the "truth" with respect to racial profiling, get used to it. This is the pervasive uncertainty governing all researchers who attempt to explain with some degree of finality whether or not a police department or individuals working for a specific police agency engage in racial profiling practices. This is largely due to the fact that data, in its very nature, is meant to "guide" researchers in their attempt to study a particular area; that is, data is not meant to be conclusive or provide arguments by its mere existence. Oftentimes, in this chapter, data seems to be inconclusive, only pointing out at a specific variable with very little or no explanation accompanying it. For instance, to say that minorities are searched more often than whites does not provide "reasons" or explanations that may help us understand better this particular trend. Thus, it is often up to the researcher or any other individual interpreting a particular data set to provide justifications or possible reasons as to why this particular phenomenon may take place. Thus, even after reviewing the fascinating findings produced in the BJS study, we continue to be haunted by the following question: How do we know racial profiling is taking place? Hopefully, the remaining chapters will continue to provide more insights that may ultimately prompt us to better understand this very complex issue.

References

Durose, R. Matthew, Schmitt, L. Erica, and Langan, A. Patrick (2005). *Contacts between Police and the Public.* Bureau of Justice Statistics. Washington, DC: U.S. Department of Justice.
New York Times "Profiling Report Leads to a Clash and a Demotion." National Desk, August 24, 2005.

CHAPTER 3

Law Enforcement: Historical and Cultural Perspectives

When we visit different news sources on the Internet or perhaps read the local paper, on most days we are likely to identify at least one story related to racial profiling. It is evident that this topic is not only sensitive to most of us but also has a tendency of being deeply divisive. In fact, it is not unusual to find people who live in the same town, neighborhood, or city block with contrasting opinions on whether or not racial profiling practices are currently taking place. Although it is clear that most of us share different opinions on this topic, the two groups with the most polarized opinions regarding racial profiling are law enforcement and civil rights advocates.

In my experience as an academic who has interacted with several hundred law enforcement agencies in the state of Texas, I have come to discover that the law enforcement community shares a common set of beliefs with regard to racial profiling, while the civil rights advocates view the issue in a very different manner. Since these two competing views are of equal value to the reader, I have decided to devote a chapter to each perspective. That is, Chapter 3 will provide a discussion on the law enforcement perspectives, while in Chapter 4 the reader will come to know the perspectives held by civil rights advocates. I hope that by doing this, the reader will recognize the value in both perspectives while understanding that we don't have to choose one over the other; rather, we can benefit from identifying the strengths of each perspective. The rationale to be used here is that by understanding both of these perspectives we will be able to better appreciate the academic, political, social, organizational, and cultural dimensions relevant to racial profiling.

The fact that the law enforcement perspective precedes the civil rights view does not suggest that one is more important than the other. Rather, as an author, I made the decision to first discuss the law enforcement perspective of racial profiling as it is clear that the civil rights position often makes reference to the law enforcement culture and organizational structure. Thus, it becomes imperative to the reader to understand certain issues in law enforcement's history and culture before reading about the civil rights perspective. Once again, these two different points of view are not presented in order of importance.

LAW ENFORCEMENT: INTRODUCTION

When we think of law enforcement, most of us envision a police officer wearing a dark-blue uniform, displaying a shinny badge, and carrying a gun with some degree of authority. We also envision images of a police officer interacting with a citizen in a professional manner, which may end with the issuance of a citation or perhaps even an arrest. However, this tendency to generalize police officers or the police culture is a far cry from accuracy. That is, law enforcement is a very complex and unique entity which is made up of individuals who—despite the fact they are encouraged, by the mere use of the same uniform and other related attributes, to act or perform similarly—all enjoy different view points regarding their role as public servants. That is, it would be an error to generalize when discussing law enforcement perspectives, particularly those related to racial profiling. That is, every chief of police, command staff member, or patrol officer is likely to have a different point of view when contemplating the manner in which racial profiling affects law enforcement. Despite the individuality of their character and perspective, there are unique and common experiences shared by law enforcement personnel that tend to offer them a unique and less individualized perspective of the world around them. Criminologists have explained this phenomenon as the "working personality," which we will discuss later on in this chapter. However, for now, just consider the fact that all officers are different but share common experiences which qualify them as belonging to the same cultural element.

I have always been amazed at the reaction by hundreds of chiefs of police when they hear my comments regarding being a minority in the United States. I start off my discussion by focusing on the experiences by members of a minority class of being stared at by everyone when they walk into a public place. When I say this, most of the class attendees, who are chiefs of police, frown in disbelief, but this quickly fades away when I tell them that being a minority is similar to being a police officer by pointing out a situation where he or she walks into a fast food place with everyone staring with curiosity or fear.

When I present this scenario to chiefs of police, some of them tell me that they finally "get it." My attempt in introducing this topic to them is to also make them realize that being a police officer parallels the experiences of members of minority groups who share the same cultural beliefs. However, it should be noted that I am not making the argument that law enforcement officers can relate, by virtue of wearing a uniform which comes off once their shift ends, with the experiences of a minority member of our community; but rather that the experiences of these two groups can be compared. In fact, if we look up the definition of "race" we find that most sources describe it as a group of people belonging to the same stock (Webster-Merriam, 2004). Therefore, the concept of race can be attributed to law enforcement personnel as well.

However, there is clearly a difference in the manner both of these groups are perceived in the scenario mentioned earlier—the officer may be perceived with fear associated with his/her official capacity, while the member of a minority group may be feared due to the perception that he or she will engage in a criminal act. This fear can have an effect on the services offered by the police. That is, members of a minority group may be rendered by the police services that are of an inferior quality when compared to those services provided to nonminorities. Despite these differences in perception, both individuals are seen as "unusual" by virtue of their appearances, which are "different" from the rest of the population. In this sense, law enforcement has the potential of relating to some of the experiences of the minority community on feeling different from the rest.

Given these similar experiences, why is it then that law enforcement personnel don't seem to relate well to minorities? Or why is it that minorities don't seem to relate well to law enforcement? Perhaps the answer to these questions can be found in the unique history, organizational structure, and cultural attributes of the law enforcement community. It will be the focus of this chapter to explore all of these components while attempting to identify the unique perspective held by the law enforcement community regarding the racial profiling issue. Doing this will hopefully provide you with a clear understanding that law enforcement personnel's perspective on racial profiling derives, to some extent, from their unique history, organizational structure, and cultural dimensions.

HISTORY

The history of policing dates back to the Roman Vigiles, the first known group of nonmilitary and nonmercenary police officers. This was formed approximately in 27 B.C. by Gaius Octavius, the grand nephew of Julius Caesar. After the assassination of Caesar, Octavius swore revenge and rose to power with the desire to reform Roman society. After becoming the ruler of Rome, he took the name *Augustus*, the first emperor of Rome (Davidson, 2000).

Among the initiatives taken by Octavius, the following are regarded as the first formalized steps toward the creation of policing:

1. Creation of a specialized unit called the *Pracetorian Guard*. These aimed to protect him from assassination. A total of 900 men were selected and divided into 9 cohorts of 100 each. Of these, 3 cohorts operated as undercover operatives housed among the civilian residents in Rome.

2. Creation of a daytime city fire brigade made up of 600 slaves. Octavius spread them among 14 separate precincts.

3. Replacement of the fire brigade with the urban cohorts. These cohorts were mediocre personnel who had not qualified to enter the Pracetorian Guard but were interested in public safety. Specifically, they were in charge of providing fire safety during daytime hours.

4. Creation of the nighttime cohorts, a supplement to the urban cohorts. The nighttime cohorts were regarded as the vigilantes or watchmen of Rome. Further, they

were authorized beyond eliminating fires. That is, they were empowered with the authority to also arrest lawbreakers. The vigilantes were armed with clubs and short swords and eventually took the duties of the urban cohorts.

In addition to the initiatives introduced by Octavius, the subsequent historical eras shaped, in one way or another, law enforcement. For instance, in the Middle Ages (A.D. 400–A.D. 1600), the predominant role of policing was related to class control. That is, police officers or those charged with the responsibility of enforcing the law were given the mission of keeping watch on vagrants or other undesirables (e.g., immigrants, gypsies, and thieves). Despite this, the Middle Ages was known as an *era of corruption* where lawlessness was abundant (Reynolds, 1926).

It is estimated that prior to 1066, the small villages of England functioned under mutual pacts, otherwise known as the *tithing system*. This particular system required that all men over the age of 12 were to form a tithing or group of individuals whose behavior was subject to the oversight of all members. The system was established in such a manner that in case a tithing failed to apprehend a suspect, all members of the tithing were required to pay restitution to the injured party. However, it was the responsibility of the chief tithingman to raise the hue and cry or "call to arms" whenever it was required to apprehend a suspect (Bopp and Schultz, 1972).

The *Frankpledge system* required for ten tithings to be organized into a "hundred," while being supervised by a constable who was typically appointed by the local nobility. The primary duty of the constable was to guard the equipment of the hundred while being able to raise forces promptly. It was typically the case that ten hundreds were further organized into a "shire" which was supervised by a "shire-reeve." The shire-reeves were regarded as the local representatives of the Norman royalty. Further, they also had judicial powers along with judges who typically traveled to hear cases. Over a period of time, the position of constable also came to represent the power of the crown. It was not until the English countrymen divided up into different parishes with aldermen and wards that the constables emerged as the most important parish officials. This was mostly due to the fact that the shire-reeves were regarded as brutal and corrupt (Bopp and Schultz, 1972).

It is clear that the law enforcement community in the United States inherits its traditions, organizational structure, and modes of operation from the English version of policing. That is, the shire-reeves became sheriffs, while towns had constables, who organized groups of watchmen, who in turn assisted in the organization of volunteers. Further, mayors usually had a high constable or marshal as their right-hand man. The U.S. criminal justice system, despite its origins in the British system, is characterized by its limited authority, decentralization, and fragmentation (Berg, 1998).

There is no doubt that the early stages of American law enforcement were based on the hue and cry model. This resulted in a silent and unseeing policing system. Boston's night watch was formed in 1631 and was the first of its kind. It consisted of six watchmen, one constable, and hundreds of volunteers. Even though professionals were compensated, unpaid volunteers did most of the work. This program was very popular to the extent that in 1652 New York City (then New Amsterdam) followed Boston's footsteps with a rattle watch. Under this particular system, patrolmen communicated with one another by shaking little wooden rattles while entering one of ten codes. In addition, the New York City police department adopted the Roman precinct system. However, in the South, things were somewhat different. That is, volunteers mostly made up the slave patrols that roamed the South. Most states in the South modeled after the Carolina colony's slave patrol of 1704. This established the notion that law enforcement officers should know every square inch of 15 square miles; that is, this system introduced the concept of "police beat" (Bopp and Schultz, 1972).

The nineteenth century prompted American police to adapt to continuous changes, most of which were social in nature. By the end of this century, police organizations ended up in the hands of politicians and big city political machines. Starting around 1835 and continuing until the 1890s, a series of industrial and race riots started to sweep the nation. Most of these involved Native Americans and Irish members of the community. Accordingly, cities responded by assigning the task of controlling the riots to police forces. However, it was not long before they discovered that the police forces mostly made up of volunteers were ill-equipped for this task. Thus, the need for salaried police officers surged.

In 1845, New York City started the paid, professional police concept. The individuals hired to protect the city were called *coppers*. This name was given after the copper stars they wore as badges on their uniforms. These officers were available, for the first time, 24 hours a day each day of the week, including Sundays. Most of the officers were from the working class, which seemed to be abundant in New York City at the time. In addition, they were armed with guns (like most people during that particular time).

The New York model was so popular that it was replicated in other cities including Philadelphia, which started the use of wanted posters depicting fugitives sought by the law. In addition, Philadelphia is known to have started a rogues gallery (mug shots). Boston was another city that sought to emulate the New York model. In Boston, police officers began to use informants, lineups, and detectives. Chicago and Detroit joined Boston and Philadelphia and adopted the paid police model. These two cities instituted rapid response via horse patrol or horse-drawn "flying squads." The rapid response initiative caught up with most Americans and soon thereafter, municipal police came to be distinctively known for this function. By 1911, all police forces were motorized and were known for their service function (Harring, 1983).

This particular historical era saw the beginning of the state and federal police agencies. At the state level, it is believed that the first state police organization was the Texas Rangers (founded in 1845). These rangers were known for their brutal acts against Comanche tribes and thousands of Mexicans. Originally, they started out as Rangers of the King, a group of henchmen for cattle baron Richard King. They were known to personify the Western motto "shoot first, ask questions later." At the federal level, the formation of agencies was prompted in part by the California Gold Rush of 1848. Some of the first federal agencies included the U.S. Postal Inspectors, Internal Revenue Service (IRS), Border Patrol, Secret Service, and the FBI. The role model for most federal agencies was Pinkerton's Private Security Agency, founded by Allan Pinkerton, a barrel maker in 1855. This particular agency was known to have interrupted strikes, secured railroads, controlled horse theft, provided military intelligence, and protected dignitaries, including presidents. It is clear that the Pinkerton security firm was present in almost every town in America. The motto "we never sleep," which was symbolized with the sign of an eye, was proudly displayed in almost every major American city. However, Pinkerton was not alone. Other companies that made a significant impact at the time included Holmes burglar alarm company, and Brinks and Wells Fargo armored truck delivery service.

The progressive era (1900–1920) witnessed significant changes in policing. The end of duties such as dog catching, inspecting, and licensing by police officers came about, while a new set of reforms were instituted. Perhaps the most significant of these involved passing the Pendleton Act (1883), which focused on the elimination of nepotism (hiring of relatives). It is clear that this era gave birth to an environment of professionalism. This was marked by the birth of the International Association of Chiefs of Police (IACP) in 1902 (Brayley, 1999).

This first president of the IACP was Richard Sylvester, chief of police in Washington DC. He was regarded as the "father of police professionalism" as he introduced a citizen-solider model. Further, Sylvester was also responsible for the development of many aspects related to the paramilitary aspect of policing. Almost at the same time Sylvester was introducing these initiatives, August Vollmer, chief of Berkeley police, became known as the "patriarch of police professionalism." This name was well earned as Vollmer introduced a more scientific manner in which police agencies conduct business. Specifically, Vollmer introduced fingerprint repositories, crime labs, and uniform reporting systems. These initiatives made the impact of transforming police departments in the United States. Most departments changed job titles, and instead of being known as *town marshals*, these individuals were called *police chiefs*. If elected, they became known as *commissioners*, and if appointed, they became known as *superintendents* (Brayley, 1999).

The evolution of police organizations was coupled with the birth of police unions (otherwise called *benevolent associations*). The Fraternal Order of Police (FOP) was created in 1915 and was soon followed by the American Federation of State County Municipal Employees (AFSCME), Teamsters, and the International Conference of Police Associations (ICPA). The development of police unions influenced members of the community to also get involved. Soon after, the Chicago Crime Commission was formed. This was a civilian oversight or review board that aimed at bringing intellectual ideas relevant to the causes of crime to policing. For the first time ever, policewomen were given the opportunity to work hand in hand with their male police counterparts and perform "real police work." Perhaps one of the most important notions that surged during this time was that higher education was important in police work and that enforcing the law was to be done in a neutral fashion (i.e., to serve and protect).

The era of the 1920s to the 1950s was largely shaped by the surge of gangsters. Al Capone, Bonnie and Clyde, Baby Face Nelson, and Machine Gun Kelly were only a few of many new notorious criminals that caught the imagination of writers and the admiration of some members of the community. Clearly, the crime-fighting mode of policing was in effect as a direct response to the threat posed by these notorious criminals. To some extent the media also helped in shaping the public perception of police officers, who were depicted in their uniforms while arresting a notorious criminal (Brayley, 1999).

The Volstead Act (otherwise known as the 18th Amendment of Prohibition) redefined the perception and role of police officers in the United States. Prohibition "changed everything." That is, it placed police officers in a role of adversaries against most citizens, who seemed to enjoy breaking the law by consuming alcohol. It was clear that the public did not want to quit its habit of consuming alcohol; therefore, the police resorted to unusual (sometimes brutal) methods to uphold prohibition laws (Brayley, 1999).

Clearly, there was a need to change the public's perception and restore its trust toward the police. At the time, two public figures emerged—J. Edgar Hoover and Elliot Ness. As most of you know, Hoover rose to the ranks of FBI director in 1924 (until 1964). Almost at the same time (in 1929), Elliot Ness, who at the time headed the Prohibition Bureau (now called ATF), also claimed fame by arresting those in violation of the prohibition laws. Historians successfully argue that both men were masters in public relations. That is, they made sure that their reputation followed them wherever they went. Those that worked for Hoover (known as the G-men) were viewed almost as being untouchable. Those that worked for Ness (known as the G-men) were also regarded in the same fashion. It was said, at the time, that those that organized crime figures often wondered, at the time, who was going to get them—the G-men or the T-men?

There were others who were equally influential in the evolution of policing. However, due to the fact they were not particularly known for their mastery in public relations, their names are now seldom recognized. These included individuals such as August Vollmer (Chief of Berkeley), O.W. Wilson (Chief of Wichita and Chicago), William Parker (Chief of Los Angeles), and William Wiltberger (Director of San Jose State University's Police School) (Bopp, 1977). Vollmer introduced the field of criminology to policing in 1941, while Wilson became the dean of criminology at Berkeley (Carte and Carte, 1975). In addition, Wiltberger founded an organization known as the National Association of College Police School Administrators, while Parker became a consultant for the television show *Dragnet*. He believed that this show would be beneficial to the public's positive perception of police officers, as he thought the show accurately portrayed the ideals he held about policing. Perhaps the most popular line of the main character of the show, "Just the facts, Ma'am," is the most appropriate example illustrating the focus of the producers on portraying a professional police force (Carte and Carte, 1975).

Although all of the individuals named earlier contributed to policing, if we were to choose one of these as the major contributor to policing, it would have to be August Vollmer. Although he did not achieve the status of a celebrity during this time, as opposed to Hoover and Ness, Vollmer made significant contributions to policing. He is known to have been responsible for the creation and implementation of stoplights, police car radios, crime labs, and lie detectors (Carte and Carte, 1975). Generally, he is considered to be an individual who held a deep conviction that policing had to rest on science. Thus, he developed scientific methodologies and applied them to common police practices. Further, Vollmer was known to have envisioned a close working relationship between academic entities and policing. Some have called Vollmer's belief that police officers should posses at least a bachelor's degree as the "college cop" movement. He took great pride in the intelligence of his police officers and was known to have made significant strides toward the introduction of women and blacks to policing. In fact, Vollmer hired the first black to work as a police officer in the United States (Carte and Carte, 1975).

Perhaps one of the most significant contributions made by Vollmer involved the drafting of the Wichersham Report. This particular report, which was mostly written by Vollmer, proposed the first baseline standards for police agencies to follow. Although this report has not transcended into accreditation standards, at the time it was believed to be revolutionary and innovative in nature (Carte and Carte, 1975). According to Walker (1977), the Wichersham Report included the following:

1. Personnel standards—removal of employees due to unacceptable behavior;
2. Communications and records—proposed modern systems based on the Berkeley model;
3. Salary and benefits schedule—fair payment schedules and promotion standards;
4. Separate units—the creation of specialized police units based on needs relevant to juvenile-related crimes or vice;
5. State information bureaus—the establishment of centers whose goals will be the collection and analysis of crime data;
6. Training academies—the creation of regional police academies.

Unfortunately, the contributions made by August Vollmer were short-lived as the United States entered the 1960s—a period of civil disorder and lack of trust on governmental institutions. In the 1960s, civil disobedience was common as Americans protested the involvement of the United States in Vietnam and, among other issues, the oppression of African Americans. The police was subject to the will of political figures who often ordered them to control (at any cost including the use of force) public gatherings of civil rights protestors. Images of police officers holding batons at the sight of civil rights activists were common. In addition, images of civil rights leaders such as Martin Luther King and Malcolm X being arrested by police officers only led toward more anger and suspicion about the role of police officers. This suspicion was materialized in the report drafted by the National Advisory Commission on Civil Disorders (1968), which became popular at the time. The report blamed the police for starting the riots. Specifically, the commission blamed the police for escalating routine traffic stops with racism and abrasiveness. It is clear today that the commission was the first known entity to publicly hold the police accountable for actions thought to be racist in nature. Although today, the analysis of traffic-stop data, which is often used in conjunction with accusations of racial profiling, is rather common, at the time, this was in fact a novelty. There is little doubt that the National Advisory Commission on Civil Disorders started, by virtue of creating its report on policing, a long held tradition of holding law enforcement accountable for actions related to racism.

The 1970s emerged with a great deal of emphasis on Police Community Relations (PCR) and similar initiatives. It became clear that PCR was an immediate concern for police departments, as private police think tanks, such as the Police Executive Research Forum (PERF), the Police Foundation, and the RAND Corporation, began to collaborate with municipal police agencies. The St. Louis Police Department became known for its innovative PCR programs including, but not limited to, Open House and Ride-Alongs. Through these outreach efforts, the police began to recognize the importance of fighting the fear of crime. Some regarded their efforts to address fear of crime as important as controlling crime itself (Walker, 1998).

One of the most notable initiatives of the 1970s was the creation of commissions to respond to pressing needs or scandals related to law enforcement. Although there are too many of these commissions to name them all, perhaps one of the most important of these was the Knapp Commission. This particular commission was influential in reminding police departments on the importance of operating internal affairs units that conducted integrity checks. This was a revolutionary concept at the time as most internal affairs units were reactive in nature. In addition, the Knapp Commission also inspired many academics to conduct research along the lines of police corruption. This commission was followed by others including the Christopher Commission, which was appointed to investigate charges of police brutality. Specifically, the Christopher Commission was asked to look into the charge that 15 police officers used excessive force against Rodney King, an African American California resident who had an exchange with police. This particular case and the commission's involvement led to efforts by social entities to look closely at racism in policing specifically, and the anthropological study of the police culture generally (Walker, 1998).

Today, policing practices also relate to sophisticated initiatives such as problem solving and community policing. These prompt police officers to interact with the public while attempting to resolve problems, some of which may require them to step out of the box and think like academics or social workers instead of law enforcers. The era of problem solving and community policing had, for the most part, been going on without much resistance or challenge. This, however, changed after the terrorist attacks of September 11, 2001. With the creation of the Department of Homeland Security and with the introduction of new security-based initiatives and responsibilities, police departments are finding it a challenge to continue to follow a community-policing philosophy within the constraints of a homeland security atmosphere. This has complicated matters even more in light of the public scrutiny that has descended on the law enforcement community with regard to racial disparities in traffic contacts and cases involving excessive use of force. The current atmosphere is complex and filled with calls for resignations and investigations (Vila and Morris, 1999).

It is not hard to understand, after reviewing the history of law enforcement, how the law enforcement community reacts to public demands calling for investigations, resignations, and in some cases, indictments of its officers in light of racist actions. The fact that the law enforcement community has witnessed many complicated and (at times) radical changes in its history gives one a sense that this is a close-knit community that does not welcome change. Further, it is a community with its own cultural realities; thus prompting police officers to belong to the same uniform code of standards and behaviors. Given this, it is appropriate to better understand the culture of law enforcement with regard to its habits and personalities. I believe that if we understand this better, we will be able to appreciate the different dimensions of racial profiling.

THE WORKING PERSONALITY AND POLICE CULTURE

In 1966, Jerome Skolnick introduced the concept of "working personality." Skolnick had always been interested in the study of police culture and had, for years, developed several models attempting to explain how police officers behaved. The working personality was born out of Skolnick's attempts to explain the effects of police deception. Specifically, Skolnick analyzed three elements that create the officer's working personality. These are danger, authority, and efficiency (Skolnick, 1966). Of these, danger is the most significant as it stimulates the development of the working personality. That is, police officers are constantly making themselves aware of who breaks the law. This results in the officer's development of suspicious behavior toward most human beings, thus, prompting them to have fewer friendships with civilians, who they may regard as potential lawbreakers.

The element of authority when combined with danger has the potential of isolating the police officer. In addition, authority has the potential of making citizens see police officers as individuals that fall outside their communities, thus, prompting police officers to feel isolated. For this attitude to develop, it does not require the officer to have a personal contact with a citizen. Regardless, most people at one time or another do have such contacts with police officers particularly in traffic-related matters. Thus, according to Skolnick, people then develop a certain image of a police officer which makes them feel as outsiders.

According to Skolnick, the working personality transcends into the daily activities of police officers. For instance, deception becomes the norm as opposed to the exception. In several instances, deception is considered by the police to be acceptable in many aspects of their job. Accordingly, a police officer learns to back up the stories told by superiors and investigators with the expectation that they will in turn back the officer up in the event this is needed—this is regarded as the "blue wall of silence" (Skolnick, 2000). According to Skolnick (2000), the blue wall of silence can often encourage officers to become violators of civil rights and involve other incidents of violence and abuse.

In addition to cautioning the reader not to draw definitive conclusions from Skolnick's work, I would offer discernment here in an attempt to make sense of the contributions made in his work. That is, although I don't personally believe that most police officers engage in deception, it is feasible to imagine that some (perhaps a few), in fact, do engage in deceptive tactics. It is clear that these individuals do not belong to police work. Thus, it is possible that the system will eventually catch up with them and they will be subsequently dismissed or prosecuted, accordingly. It should also be mentioned that Skolnick wrote the working personality theory in the 1960s; thus, many of his inferences were based on his observations of police work then (and not now). Therefore, his conclusions are a bit dated and not directly relevant to contemporary policing practices.

Nevertheless, it is important to recognize that Skolnick's main contribution (the development of the working personality concept) is interesting and insightful, particularly the aspect related to the isolation of officers. Those of us who have worked, at one time or another, with police officers can attest to the fact that the dynamics of the policing culture are alive and well. That is, police officers belong to a culture often known for its cynical humor and blunt approach to most issues.

My first exposure to the working personality was during my senior year in college. A good friend of mine who was a police officer in south Florida asked me to serve as the best man for his upcoming wedding. Naturally, he had planned a bachelor's party with his friends from the police department and had invited me to be part of the event as well. The party would take place at his house, where his wife to be would also hold a similar event with her girlfriends. When I showed up in his house, I was amazed to see that most of his friends were gathered around several coolers filled with ice and beer. They were loud and seemed to be enjoying themselves while telling stories about what appeared to be contacts with the so-called *bad guy* (term used often by law enforcement officers when referring to criminals). I noticed, though, that as soon as I showed up and said hello to my friend, all of the storytellers and members of the crowd became quiet as they looked at me with suspicion. One of them asked my friend if I was *legit* (term used to describe if individual is crime free or legitimate). When my friend said, "Yes, Alex is legit," they all continued laughing and telling their stories related to their encounters with the bad guy. At the time I did not think much of this incident. However, years later, I recognized that I had personally witnessed the working personality.

The working personality is relevant to the study of racial profiling as it relates to the culture in which police officers operate on a daily basis when interacting with the public. Further, it provides an insight into the possible expectations that police officers may have toward citizens in general and minorities in particular. In other words, does the working personality and overall sense of suspicion experienced by officers give rise to a belief, among some officers, that minorities are most likely to commit crimes? If true, this could transcend to a predisposition, on behalf of police officers, to issue a citation, use force, or arrest individuals thought to be most likely to engage in criminality.

Given what we have studied so far about the evolution of labeling and profiling in the United States and the manner in which minorities were treated, it is no wonder that we have public outcries demanding justice toward police-initiated actions. Restated, when police officers interact with members of minority groups, the police culture, in which suspicion of others is a feature, meets eye to eye with the culture of minorities, who are, by their own historical accounts, suspicious of law enforcers—thus giving rise to a significantly higher number of racial profiling claims. Given this, perhaps the better question to ask is, Why aren't there any more instances where police and minorities clash?

ORGANIZATIONAL STRUCTURE

Most police departments are militaristic in nature. That is, the organizational structure, attire (i.e., uniforms), rituals, and traditions are based on a military tradition. Particularly in organizational structure, much in the same manner as the military, police departments enjoy from a chain of command. Typically, at the top of the chain is the decision maker who sets the tone for the department. That is, the chief of police represents the highest authority in a police department. This individual typically enjoys from having several assistant chiefs responsible for different components of the department, including, but not limited to, the uniform patrol division, investigative function, and/or internal affairs.

Assistant chiefs are assisted by deputy chiefs, captains, or commanders depending on the needs or organizational structure of a specific department. These high-level supervisors are assisted by lieutenants, who are primarily responsible for specific beats or subdivisions. Lieutenants are, in turn, assisted by sergeants or mid-level supervisors who typically have daily contacts with officers. The sergeants are meant to facilitate the police department to function without much controversy or difficulty. Sadly, this is not always the case as in some instances sergeants have very little contact with their officers due to the administrative duties that they attend to. The last component in the chain of command is the individual officer. It is the individual patrol officer who, regardless of his/her limited authority and power within the chain of command, likely enjoys a great deal of independence. As a chief of police once told me, "I truly envy patrol officers; they simply clock out of their shift and go home; they then forget they are officers until the next time they are due to go back to work. We, chiefs of police, are on duty 24 hours a day/7 days a week. You cannot escape the responsibility of being chief even when you go away on a trip. You are always on call!"

As in the military, officers seldom speak or even see the chief of police. They receive notices from the chief via the chain of command; typically, the chief's directives are read to the officers before the start of their shift. Today, there are police departments in existence whose chiefs do not know most of its officers. Thus, in some cases, where the number of officers exceeds 5,000, it is common to find that chiefs have to print the officer's picture and biography in an attempt to learn more about the individual's assignment and work history before meeting with the officer.

Thus, there is, at times, a true disconnect between the opinion of a patrol officer and a member of the command staff, particularly the chief. I found that in my interactions with police departments, members of the patrol division would share with me, in confidence, their perception regarding the department's declining standards and weak leadership. However, when speaking to members of the command staff, I found that their perspective would be entirely different. In fact, they would often argue that "things were great" and that the department was in its best years.

This apparent disconnect is worth mentioning here as it is imperative to explore the perspective of police chiefs and patrol officers toward racial profiling. Although, as you will realize in the subsequent sections, they share similar concerns, there are instances where the opinions and perspectives vary with regard to this topic. That is, chiefs see this topic as one that can easily end their careers whereas officers view it as a concept alien to them since they don't feel their role as officers allows them to be anything but fair and ethical.

CHIEFS' PERSPECTIVE

Although there is a clear absence of empirical data in the academic literature with regard to the perspective of police chiefs toward racial profiling, it has become clear to me, after interacting with more than 1,200 chiefs of police, that most of them share similar views—they view racial profiling as a direct threat to their tenure as chiefs of police.

As we discuss the perspective of police chiefs toward racial profiling, it is important to remember that police officers in general, are, by virtue of their own job, often paranoid about hidden agendas that organizations may have regarding policing in general. That is, although it may be hard for a member outside the police community to believe that there is a secret agenda behind the actions of a civil rights group, for police officers in general, this is a widely acceptable notion. In my conversations with chiefs of police, it became clear to me that most of them believe that "liberals" are trying to destroy the core values of the "American" way of life by virtue of their efforts to impair the ability of law enforcement to perform their duties.

That is, racial profiling, according to chiefs, is yet another issue that has become grossly politicized. I should note that I have yet to have a conversation with a chief of police who believes that racism does not exist. In fact, in the course of my interaction with chiefs, I have often heard comments about fellow officers they had known in their careers whom they qualified as "not belonging in law enforcement." Also, I have never heard anyone say to me that they had encouraged their officers to racially profile an individual. In fact, I often heard chiefs express, with some degree of passion, their dislike for individuals who make "the rest of us look bad."

Even if you don't particularly believe that most chiefs of police are not racist, it is hard to imagine that anyone in this position today would not have any regard for his/her career and encourage subordinates to profile. Being a chief of police today, I argue, involves expecting a "bad day from being a former chief." It is clear to me and to the chiefs with whom I have held long conversations that racial profiling can quickly produce the "bad day" they fear will end their career and tenure.

The concerns expressed by chiefs are almost the same across the board. Perhaps the most popular concern is that they feel racial profiling is an issue they can "never win." That is, they feel that regardless of their actions, the perception held by the public regarding this topic, coupled with the perspective encouraged by media reports based on aggregate reports, makes racial profiling a no-win situation for them. In the words of one chief, "racial profiling is like a locomotive that can end my career and I cannot do anything to stop it." Most chiefs have expressed their dislike for figures on racial profiling as they feel these have a tendency of allowing departments and their officers to be judged before they have an opportunity to defend their case.

The second area of concern has to do with funding. That is, during times when every dollar is often micromanaged by city managers and council members, police chiefs often find that they don't have the resources to hire outside assistance to help them comply with state laws regarding profiling issues. That is, it is often the case that police chiefs, once they become aware of the potential liability of racial profiling, are encouraged by their own instincts of self-preservation to hire outside consulting firms which can help them be in compliance with state laws and assist them in the analysis of traffic-stop data. However, city managers, who are often blinded and ignorant of this topic, express a disregard and lack of support for paying high-dollar consultants to assist them. As I have found, it takes for someone to mention the word "liability" for city officials to all of a sudden become "interested" in the topic. This is particularly true when they become aware that most racial profiling lawsuits have been filed in small cities in the United States. At the point of realization, when city officials understand the potential liability of racial profiling, they express support to the local chief, who in turn becomes relieved that he/she will have the opportunity to comply with the law, while increasing the chances of remaining employed.

Another concern often held by chiefs of police is that citizens in a community at large seldom understand the concept of racial profiling. That is, police officers are, at times, called in by citizens complaining to the 911 operator that a "suspicious man is walking in my neighborhood." When asked by the operator what makes this man suspicious, the callers often say, "well, you know, very few black people live here and this guy is black so clearly he has no business here." Although a sad reality, this type of call is often made to police departments nationwide. Chiefs of police argue that their responsibility is to respond to this call regardless of their belief that the presence of a black man in a particular neighborhood is not illegal and does not require a police response.

Although I am not trying to encourage the reader to believe that all police chiefs are individuals who share the view of "equality for all," it is clear to me, based on my experiences with chiefs of police, that most of them value their job and understand that the absence of action and data analysis relevant to profiling measures can result in their termination. Being a chief of police is, for the most part, a very isolating experience and can result in the complete disconnect of police chiefs from the rest of the officers. Sadly, this takes place more often than not as patrol officers often view chiefs as CEOs that forgot the meaning of true police work.

OFFICERS' PERSPECTIVE

The perspective of patrol officers is quite different from those shared by chiefs of police. For the most part, patrol officers are individuals that often regard racial profiling as "nonsense." Many of them simply don't see the point in collecting traffic-contact data in an attempt to determine if they engage in profiling. That is, they don't understand why there is a skeptic public eagerly awaiting to formulate an opinion, one away or another, regarding the department's racial profiling tendencies.

It is clear that police work is often associated with the exposure to dimensions of humanity that are seldom witnessed by the rest of us. Clearly, most police officers, by virtue of their trade, are aware of acts of violence and other related circumstances that depict the worst behavior of human beings. One would think, based on this, that most police officers would not be naive when discussing racial profiling. The opposite is true. Sadly, they appear to hold a naive attitude toward racial profiling in general. It is often the case that they (patrol officers) don't understand why anyone would question their authority and actions given the fact that, in their view, they are simply "not racist."

Patrol officers, oftentimes, ignore the history and contemporary issues related to racism. Some of them, in fact, believe that the data collection requirement imposed on their department is nothing more than a fragment of the imagination of the chief of police, who seems to be almost always ready to "make their lives impossible." In fact, some of them are convinced that initiatives regarding racial profiling data collection have been designed and implemented by the chief of police in his/her attempt to gain public support and recognition for being innovative.

The patrol officers' reaction to such initiatives should not surprise us. Some of them, such as those working for the city of Houston, Texas, decided, when faced with the racial profiling data requirement, that they would simply cease to issue as many citations as in prior instances. The decline of citations became apparent and it ended up affecting the revenue of the city. It was not until months after the requirement was passed that it was apparent that officers reengaged traffic in the same manner as in prior instances.

For many patrol officers, the requirement to record traffic-stop data is nothing more than a waste of time. In fact, I often heard them complain that "recording racial profiling data takes away from me the necessary time I need to devote to community policing practices." Others claimed that they joined the police force to become crime fighters and not statisticians.

Perhaps one of the most damaging complaints voiced by patrol officers relates to the notion held by many of them that they have already been convicted by public opinion regarding racial profiling; thus, they feel no need to collect data related to this issue. In fact, many of them claim not to understand aggregate data analysis but feel that the data they record and subsequently produce to the public has the effect of reinforcing the public's negative view of law enforcement.

Despite this, it should be noted that some patrol officers feel that collecting racial profiling data is not only mandatory but it is a necessity in order to show transparency before the community. Even though they are obviously a minority, it is important to acknowledge that they are in fact, in agreement with the idea that racial profiling should be measured and addressed, if necessary. Perhaps most of us would assume that these officers are for the most part members of a minority group; however, this is not necessarily the case.

It should be noted that minority officers often find themselves with mixed feelings about racial profiling. Their fellow minority members of the community pose this question to them—"Do you still remember what it's like to be black or did you forget this at the police academy?" Interestingly, they are challenged to demonstrate their loyalty to their own ethnicity or race by giving a suspect a break. However, if they decide to abide by their obligations and proceed with the enforcement of the law, they are regarded as minorities who have abandoned their own ethnicity or race and have now joined the "class of blue." During my conversations with minority patrol officers, they often mentioned that they knew that racial profiling was taking place from personal experience. They noted instances where they were out of uniform and were subsequently pulled over by fellow police officers who ignored the fact that they were law enforcement agents. Interestingly, while setting aside their own experiences, they were quick to point out that their own departments were not engaging in racial profiling; in their view, it was clearly a problem in other departments but their own.

Regardless of how patrol officers may feel about the concept of racial profiling, most of them agree that they dislike the idea of having "big brother" watching over their shoulder regarding contacts made with citizens. In fact, some of them believe that the department of internal affairs and other groups within police agencies seem to constantly review the racial profiling figures in an attempt to "get one of them in trouble." It is not hard to imagine that police officers would feel this way given the unique cultural characteristics of policing.

OVERALL PERSPECTIVES ON PROFILING

The history of law enforcement, as you have read earlier on in this chapter, is very complex. The professionalization of policing is a rather new phenomenon. The idea that police officers are college-educated professionals who strive to provide the best possible service to a complex community is the norm in some departments in the United States. Nevertheless, the law enforcement culture is often portrayed as being unique and complex. This culture is particularly affected when contemplating the issue of racial profiling. It is often the case that chiefs of police feel that this issue can end their career while patrol officers regard racial profiling as an "evil" that seeks to destroy and undermine their authority as enforcers of the law.

It is clear from the points introduced in this discussion that racial profiling has found, in the law enforcement community, a cold reception in a skeptical audience. The idea that this concept can enhance the noble ideals which may have once influenced a police officer to become a law enforcement agent is simply not the case. Instead, racial profiling adds suspicion to an already-present skepticism of the audience. This results in a more divisive attitude which tends to isolate police officers even more; thus, engaging the public while practicing an "us" versus "them" attitude. Ironically, this attitude may give rise to more incidents of racial profiling and more hostile interactions with minorities. Thus, racial profiling initiatives not only fail to carry out their mission of achieving transparency and awareness of a growing minority civilian population; it also gives rise to feelings of frustration which often result in negative attitudes toward the public.

References

Brayley, D. (1999). "The Development of Modern Police," in L. Gaines and G. Cordner (eds.) *Policing Perspectives: An Anthology*. Los Angeles: Roxbury, pp. 59–78.

Berg, B. (1998). *Law Enforcement: An Introduction to Police in Society*. Boston: Allyn and Bacon.

Bopp, W. (1977). *O.W. Wilson and the Search for a Police Profession*. Port Washington, NY: Kennikat Press.

Bopp, W. and D. Schultz (1972). *A Short History of American Law Enforcement*. Springfield: Charles Thomas.

Carte, G. and E. Carte (1975). *Police Reform in the United States: The Era of August Vollmer*. Berkeley: University of California Press.

Davidson, J.M. (2000). *Derecho e Ideologia en la Roma Tardo-Republicana*. Pomoerium 4–5.

Harring, S. (1983). *Policing a Class Society: The Experience of American Cities, 1865–1915*. New Brunswick: Rutgers University Press.

Reynolds, P. (1926). *The Vigiles of Imperial Rome*. London: Oxford University Press.

Skolnick, Jerome H. (1966). *Justice Without Trial*. New York: John Wiley and Sons Inc.

Skolnick, Jerome H. (2000). "Code Blue." *The American Prospect*. Vol. 11, No. 10. March 27–April 10.

Vila, B. and C. Morris (1999). *The Role of Police in American Society: A Documentary History*. Westport: Greenwood Press.

Walker, S. (1977). *A Critical History of Police Reform*. Lexington: Lexington Books.

Walker, S. (1998). *Police in America*. New York: McGraw-Hill.

Webster-Merriam (2004). Webster Dictionary.

CHAPTER 4

Civil Rights and Racial Profiling

INTRODUCTION

It is inconceivable to write a book on racial profiling without discussing the slavery and civil rights eras and their impact on race relations in the United States. In this chapter, I will not attempt to provide comprehensive views or notions regarding slavery or the civil rights period. Instead, I hope to provide the reader with a sense of the slavery period and the civil rights struggle and its current mission as it relates to racial profiling.

The history of the civil rights movement in the United States has been the subject of many academic discussions and forums. In these discussions, it has become clear that the "struggle for freedom" arrived at the cost of human sacrifice and struggle. In the eve of the passing of Rosa Parks, we are reminded of the courage expressed by amazing individuals who faced off the challenges associated with racism. The history of the civil rights movement is in itself the story of human courage and struggle. It is also the story of ignorance personified by individuals who, by virtue of their own insecurities, felt that they were biologically superior to other races, particularly blacks. Today, most of us agree that the civil rights struggle is deeply associated with the current issues affecting race relations in the United States, with racial profiling being one of the most pressing race-related issues today. Thus, in order to understand racial profiling from all perspectives, we shall now deal with the history of slavery, the civil rights movement, its struggle, the evolution of civil rights organizations such as the American Civil Liberties Union (ACLU), the National Association for the Advancement of Colored People (NAACP), and the League of United Latin American Citizens (LULAC), and the current civil rights perspectives and campaigns focusing on racial profiling.

THE HISTORY OF SLAVERY

Historians argue that the struggle for civil rights started before the Civil War in the United States. That is, according to Thomas (2006), blacks had fought for their rights of expression and free will in the Northern states prior to the Civil War between the Southern states (Confederacy) and the Northern/Western states (Union). As a result of their efforts, blacks had won some independence in the Northern states, which led to the desire of some Southern blacks to escape to the North. One of these black slaves was Frederick Baily (later Frederick Douglass). Frederick Baily was born in 1818 on Holmes Hill Farm, near the town of Easton on Maryland's Eastern Shore (Thomas, 2006). He grew up with his grandmother as his mother was forced into slavery early on in his childhood. Frederick struggled with slavery, and although most of his learning was self-taught, using his gift to charm those around him, at a young age he charmed one of his masters to teach him the alphabet. Sadly, this particular attribute did not prevent him from being subject, as other slaves, to regular beatings and other related abuses. As he planned to escape to the North, he changed his name from Frederick Baily to Frederick Douglass. At some point in his early teenage years, Frederick managed to escape to the Northern free-states and eventually made his way to New York City, where he felt inexpressible joy realizing he had finally achieved the freedom he desired since early childhood. He later wrote, "A new world had opened upon me. Anguish and grief, like darkness and rain, may be depicted, but gladness and joy, like the rainbow, defy the skill of pen or pencil" (Thomas, 2006). In New York City, he married, had two children, and continued to read materials related to slavery. It was in New York where Douglass began to actively seek out movements whose aim was to abolish slavery (Thomas, 2006). Naturally, he joined the abolitionists (a group whose main goal was to abolish slavery). Douglass developed a talent for public speaking and eventually became one of the most important anti-slavery figures of the nineteenth century. In fact, he is regarded as the key player in the acceleration of the opposition to slavery in the years leading to the Civil War of 1861–1865 (Huggins, 1980).

The Abolitionists

The abolitionists were individuals who were concerned with abolishing slavery. In December 1833, these individuals, under the principal organizers William Lloyd Garrison and Arthur and Lewis Tappan, formed the American Anti-Slavery Society in Philadelphia. They were responsible for publishing in 1831 the *Liberator*, an abolitionist journal (Columbia Electronic Encyclopedia, 2006). The main goal of the society was to denounce slavery as a moral evil, while calling for the immediate release of slaves (Columbia Electronic Encyclopedia, 2006). In 1835, the society launched a significant propaganda campaign by flooding states that were predominantly affected by slavery with literature that encouraged the freedom of slaves. Members of the society were sent to the North to organize state and local antislavery societies, and they petitioned the U.S. Congress for the abolition of slavery in the District of Columbia.

Because of their efforts and organization, the abolitionists were met with much resistance. Specifically, they were first denounced and abused while mobs attacked them in the North. The South was much more violent in resisting the abolitionists' petitions. Reports were filed indicating that Southerners burned antislavery pamphlets and in some areas prevented abolitionists from utilizing mail services. The federal government did not respond any kinder when compared to the North or South. In fact, the U.S. Congress imposed a gag order as a means to avoid considering the petition filed by them (Columbia Electronic Encyclopedia, 2006). This, added to the murder of abolitionist editor Elijah P. Lovejoy in 1837, led to the fear that the constitutional rights of all would not be observed. The widespread fear that constitutional rights would be ignored was used by the abolitionists as a tool to gather support. As a result, they successfully attained enough support that by 1838, more than 1,350 antislavery societies existed with a membership of almost 250,000 members, including a rather large representation of women (Columbia Electronic Encyclopedia, 2006).

Most abolitionists agreed that their first priority and objective should be the abolition of slavery. However, despite this common goal, some disagreed regarding the means to achieve this goal. Specifically, Garrison believed in moral suasion as the only means to achieve complete success. This, added to Garrison's belief that women should participate in all events related to the antislavery society, angered the conservative members of the group. Despite this resistance, those who followed Garrison managed to pass this resolution in the 1840 convention, and as a consequence a large group led by the Tappan brothers withdrew from this organization, while forming the American and Foreign Anti-Slavery Society. This particular event led to the departure of other members from the society. In turn, the struggle for the freedom of slaves was transformed to the lecture platform (Schneider and Schneider, 2001).

ANTI-SLAVERY SOCIETY

Some of the strongest individuals who had supported the American Anti-Slavery Society began to take leadership roles by founding other political action groups. For instance, advocates of direct political action founded the Liberty Party in 1840 (Schneider and Schneider, 2001). In fact, James G. Birney was the party's presidential candidate in 1840 and again in 1844. Other supporters included writers such as John Greenleaf Whittier and orators such as Wendell Phillips, who frequently offered their services and intellectual contributions toward slave freedom. These intellectuals were also joined by freed slaves such as Frederick Douglass, who also took his fight to the lecture platform.

As a result of these particular individual efforts, an antislavery lobby was created in 1842. Its influence and power grew as abolitionists, who supported this lobbying effort, hoped to convert the South through the churches. These hopes were extinguished soon after religious groups in the South such as the Methodists in 1844 and the Baptists in 1845 announced their withdrawal from their Northern brethren (Schneider and Schneider, 2001).

Soon after the collapse of the Liberty Party, the abolitionists began to support the Free Soil Party. This particular party prompted abolitionists to vote in 1856 for the

Republican Party. Once again, abolitionists saw a change in the means used to fight slavery. The passage of more stringent fugitive slave laws in 1850 increased their activity in the Underground Railroad, a route through which slaves escaped to freedom (Cozzens, 1997).

THE UNDERGROUND RAILROAD

The Underground Railroad was described as a "network of paths through the woods and fields, river crossings, boats and ships, trains and wagons, all haunted by the specter of recapture" (Blockson, 1984). Perhaps no other name is associated more often with the Underground Railroad than *Harriet Tubman* (a.k.a. *Moses*). Harriet Tubman was born into slavery in Maryland in 1819 or 1820 and was often beaten as a child (Cozzens, 1997). At the age of 12 she was injured by a blow to the head that was inflicted by a white overseer for refusing to tie a slave who had attempted to escape. Harriet grew up with a conviction that she should live in a free society. At the age of 25 she married John Tubman, a free African American, and five years later, fearing she would be sold to the South, she escaped to Canada. She based her operations in Canada and from there she assisted the movement to free other slaves, including members of her family. While escaping slavery, Harriet discovered the Underground Railroad system, which she later assisted with irrevocable conviction. In fact, she was often cited as saying that God would assist her in rescuing slaves and moving them through the Underground Railroad (Cozzens, 1997). And in the event rescued slaves changed their mind and tried to end their journey to freedom early, thus, endangering the identity of those individuals who assisted in their rescue efforts, Harriet always carried a shotgun prepared to shoot the slave who would betray her efforts. She became known as the *Moses* of slaves and was a pioneer in the efforts to free slaves.

The Underground Railroad derived its name from the following incident that occurred in 1831:

> [A fugitive named Tice Davids came over the line and lived just back of Sandusky.] When he was running away, his master, a Kentuckian, was in close pursuit and pressing him so hard that when the Ohio River was reached he had no alternative but to jump in and swim across. It took his master some time to secure a skiff, in which he and his aid followed the swimming fugitive, keeping him in sight until he had landed. Once on shore, however, the master could not find him. . . . [A]fter a long search the disappointed slave-master went into Ripley, and when inquired of as to what has become of his slave, said . . . he thought "the nigger must have gone off on an underground road" (Schneider and Schneider, 2001).

This incident gave the name to the line. First, it was called the *Underground Road* and later it became known as the *Underground Railroad* (Smedley, 1883, pp. 34, 35).

This particular effort was also made possible by courageous men and women who were determined to preserve the rights of all humans, including those that were persecuted and tortured. The work of the Underground Railroad was tough and dangerous. Oftentimes, secret codes using railroad jargon alerted "passengers" when traveling was adequate or safe. Typically, escapees would either travel alone or in small groups and were typically assisted by African American and white "conductors" or individuals who operated the Underground Railroad. Some of these conductors made a name for themselves and today they are recognized for their valiant cause. One of them was James Fairfield, who was a white abolitionist who went into the Deep South to rescue enslaved African Americans. He posed as a slave trader in order to acquire, transport, and free slaves. Another noteworthy conductor was John Parker, an African American abolitionist from Ripley, Ohio. He was known to frequently venture to Kentucky and Virginia to help transport (by boat) hundreds of escapees across the Ohio River. Perhaps the closest the Underground Railroad came to being formally organized was during the 1830s, at a time when African American abolitionists William Still, Robert Purvis, David Ruggles, and others began to organize and station vigilance committees. These committees were deployed throughout the North in order to assist bondsmen to escape to freedom. It is estimated that between 1810 and 1850 a total of 100,000 slaves escaped the South via the Underground Railroad (Schneider and Schneider, 2001).

THE CIVIL WAR

On November 6, 1860, Abraham Lincoln was elected as president of the United States. A strong abolitionist, he once expressed his views on the topic as follows: "Government cannot endure permanently half slave, half free . . ." Lincoln was known, prior to his election as president of the United States, for his intellectual ability and ideological opposition to slavery. Specifically, he supported the notion that the federal government had the authority to limit slavery among the states. This was included in his Cooper Union Speech, which was delivered in New York City prior to his election as president (Schneider and Schneider, 2001).

Lincoln's presidency was filled with pain and sorrow. This was mostly due to the fact that the country was divided between those that advocated for slavery and those that opposed it. Mostly, the Southern states believed that slavery was their right and that their economic stability depended on it. On the other hand, the Northern states, who were largely influenced by the religious beliefs of the Quakers, adhered to the notion that slavery should not be tolerated. Thus, the Civil War commenced. It is estimated that approximately 3 million fought during the Civil War and a total of 600,000 died. The Civil War started in 1861 and ended in 1865 (Mellon, 1988). Despite the fact that the war ended with the victory of the North, which enabled the freedom of slaves, the challenges related to racism in the United States did not end then. Thousands of freed slaves celebrated their freedom with much enthusiasm without the knowledge of the events that would soon follow which depicted the reality that freedom from slavery did not necessarily mean equality for all.

POST–CIVIL WAR ERA AND BLACK CODES

Soon after the Civil War ended, recently freed slaves found themselves with a system of government that allowed for the segregation of communities based on racial demographics. This was also accompanied by the denial to vote in any election and humiliation which became evident as African Americans were obliged to drink from their own (segregated) water fountains. However, life for blacks after the war was not bad for some. In fact, some blacks experienced a form of economic advancement particularly in the catering business. Perhaps the most significant advancement of blacks after the war was related to education and schooling. With the assistance of the North and a few organizations that were concerned primarily in the academic advancement of blacks—the American Missionary Association and the Freedman's Bureau—they were able to attain an education. For some, this meant the ability to read and write. Clearly, this also meant that blacks were becoming more aware of academic disciplines, some of which related to their newly acquired rights. People in the South perceived the academic advancement of blacks as a threat; they felt that blacks would become "too independent" and would learn to "hate the south" as they reflected on the slavery years (Schneider and Schneider, 2001).

The Civil War marked the end of slavery but geographic boundaries with respect to the treatment of blacks continued. That is, blacks in the South were still beaten and humiliated in a manner comparable to the treatment they received prior to the Civil War. For instance, blacks in Southern states were not allowed to "talk back" or engage in any disrespectful act against whites. When they encountered a white person, they were required to come to attention until the white person left the area. People in the South established the Black Codes; these aimed at limiting the opportunities for blacks. Primarily, the Black Codes required that blacks did not look for "better jobs" or sought any advancement in their career (Schneider and Schneider, 2001). Also, the Codes required that blacks maintain a job at all times; if a black worker was found unemployed, he/she would be charged with vagrancy. The idea was to limit the amount of freedom exercised by blacks. This was particularly true among individuals who sought to be self-sufficient. For instance, the Black Codes prohibited blacks from raising their own crops or engaging in any behavior that would result in them being considered self-sufficient. The Codes also limited their mobility to the extent that if a black man/woman was caught in a different town or city without papers from their employer, which would specify the length of stay and reason for visiting, they would end up in jail (Schneider and Schneider, 2001).

THE FOURTEENTH AMENDMENT

The Black Codes remained in effect until 1866, when the federal court declared them too harsh. Further, the Court affirmed that blacks should receive the same treatment as whites, including being accorded similar rights and responsibilities. This clearly ended for blacks the harsh era which followed the Civil War. For once, blacks were able to roam around and begin exploring possibilities of advancement. This did not come easy and was due, in large part, to the sacrifice of whites and blacks who fought hand in hand for the liberty from oppression of all blacks, particularly those in the South (Schneider and Schneider, 2001).

In 1867, the Fourteenth Amendment of the U.S. Constitution was passed by Congress. This particular amendment was designed to grant citizenship to blacks, as well as protect their civil rights. As could be expected, Southern states refused to ratify this amendment; this led radical Republicans such as Thaddeus Stevens, Charles Sumner, Benjamin Wade, Henry Winter Davies, and Benjamin Butler to pass further legislation that aimed at imposing these measures in the former confederacy (Mellon, 1988).

The U.S. Congress was at odds with Andrew Johnson, the president of the United States. President Johnson had been quoted as saying that as long as he was president he would make it clear that the United States was for whites only as they constituted a superior race when compared to blacks. Clearly, his deeds spoke louder than his words as he vetoed just about every bill that was passed in the Congress demanding the rights and equal treatment of blacks (Cozzens, 1997).

THE FIRST RECONSTRUCTION ACT

On March 2, 1867, the U.S. Congress passed the first Reconstruction Act, which divided the South into five military districts, each under the supervision of a major general. With the passage of the new act, elections in which freed male slaves would vote for the first time were to be held in all Southern states. The Act also contained language allowing for Southern states to be readmitted to the Union after they had ratified the Fourteenth Amendment. Despite the fact President Johnson vetoed the recently passed bill, Congress repassed it the same day (Schneider and Schneider, 2001).

It became clear soon that the Southern states would rather live under a military rule than ratify the Fourteenth Amendment. This prompted Congress to pass a supplementary Reconstruction Act on March 23; it authorized the military commanders to supervise elections and generally to provide the support needed to create new governments. As in previous instances, President Johnson vetoed the act on the grounds that it interfered with the right of every citizen to be left to the free exercise of his own judgment when he is engaged in the work of forming a fundamental law. The first two Reconstruction Acts were followed by numerous supplementary acts passed by Congress; these provided the military with the authority to register the voters and supervise the elections. As a result of these measures, all of the Southern states returned to the Union by 1870.

THE CIVIL RIGHTS MOVEMENT

Despite the fact that blacks had come a long way from the years of slavery, challenges still remained in place with regard to civil rights and principles of equality. Differences related to pay, work, education, health care, and overall living conditions prevailed from the 1870s until the early 1950s. Schools were segregated and social conditions for blacks were deplorable. The voices advocating the freedom and equality of blacks of the Civil War era were far gone and all that remained was confusion and despair. The late 1940s were surrounded by racial conflict and the struggle for equal rights (Schneider and Schneider, 2001). Although it is beyond the scope of this book, it should be noted that at the time of this racial conflict in the United States, the struggle to fight discrimination against women was also in place. This ultimately led to the National Women's Party, which was responsible for the enactment of the Equal Rights Amendment.

In 1947, the Congress of Racial Equality (CORE) planned a "Journey of Reconciliation" designed to challenge existing case law with respect to segregated seating of interstate passengers unconstitutional. An interracial group of passengers met with a great deal of resistance in the South; they later served on a chain gang after they were arrested in North Carolina. Clearly, the South, including the most moderate upper South, were not ready for integration (Schneider and Schneider, 2001).

THE MONTGOMERY BUS BOYCOTT

It was clear that drastic action by all members of civil rights groups was required. The Montgomery Bus Boycott officially started on December 1, 1955 (Cozzens, 1997). This was the day when the blacks of Montgomery, Alabama, decided that they would boycott the city buses until they were granted the right to sit anywhere they wished. The traditional practice was for blacks to sit in the back of the bus when a white person boarded. The boycott originated from the courage of a seamstress named Rosa Parks who in 1943 refused to give up her seat for a white passenger.

ROSA PARKS

On Thursday, December 1, 1955, Rosa Parks boarded a city bus and sat along with three other blacks in the fifth row of the bus (Cozzens, 1997). This was the first row in the bus that was occupied by blacks. A few stops later, the front four rows became filled with white passengers. However, one white passenger remained standing as all other seats were occupied. According to the law at the time, blacks and whites could not occupy the same row. So the bus driver demanded that all four of the blacks seated in the fifth row should move to allow the white passenger, who remained standing, to occupy a seat. As history recorded the events of the day, all blacks complied with the demands of the bus driver except one—Rosa Parks. As a result, Rosa Parks was arrested and jailed for failing to adhere to the law (Williams, 1987). Although Rosa Parks is now known as the most significant historical character of the Bus Boycott era, there is more to the story regarding her contributions to the civil rights movement. A little-known fact is that Rosa Parks was educated; she attended the laboratory school at Alabama State College since there was no high school for blacks in Montgomery at the time. She had decided to become a seamstress since she could not find a job that would be commensurate with the skills she learned in school. She was also a long-time NAACP worker.

THE MONTGOMERY IMPROVEMENT ASSOCIATION

After being arrested, a lawyer approached Rosa Parks and asked for her permission to bring her case to the courts in an attempt to stop segregation in buses. After reflecting on this opportunity, Rosa Parks agreed. This not only initiated a legal battle which questioned segregation but also gave rise to a movement across the United States which demanded for equality. In fact, soon after Park's arrest, Jo Ann Robinson, a civil rights activist, began to plan a one-day boycott of all buses. She created and distributed hand-outs asking blacks to stay off city buses on Monday—the day Park's case was going to be considered before the court. Robinson's efforts to plan a boycott were aided by the ministers who encouraged all attendees of the church on Sunday to participate in the boycott. Dr. Martin Luther King, Jr., who was minister at Dexter Avenue Baptist Church, thought that if "we could get 60 percent cooperation the protest would be a success" (Williams, 1987). According to Dr. King, a miracle had occurred as the "once dormant and quiescent Negro community was now fully awake." The group that met on Friday night met again that afternoon and achieved consensus that they should call themselves the Montgomery Improvement Association (MIA). They opted to name Dr. King as president of their association. Although the MIA considered ending the boycott at the end of the day, the membership was asked to vote on the issue and the majority decided that they should continue with the boycott for an indefinite amount of time.

DESEGREGATION PLANS

On December 8, only a few days after the boycott had been initiated, the leadership of MIA met with the bus company and attempted at resolving the matter by proposing a desegregation plan similar to the one in place in cities such as Mobile, Alabama. After considering all possible angles and perspectives, the bus company decided against the proposal and in fact went a step beyond the earlier stance by enforcing a rule that prompted cab drivers to charge no less than a 45-cent fare. It should be mentioned that black cab drivers had been charging only 10 cents a ride to help their fellow black citizens to manage during the boycott (Cozzens, 1997).

Faced with the prospect that thousands of blacks would not have a mode of transportation to get to work, the MIA designed a "private taxi" plan, which prompted blacks who owned cars to pick up and drop off blacks who needed rides. The plan required an unprecedented amount of effort and coordination. However, it worked so well that even the white groups supporting desegregation had to admit that the plan worked with "military precision" (Cozzens, 1997).

Once faced with the reality that the boycott would not end, white groups began to launch aggressive methods to end the strike. Their first tactic included the division of blacks by proposing terms to a few ministers unaffiliated with the protest, which was later mischaracterized as a settlement with the protestors. The idea was to misinform and confuse the black population. This went so far that all newspapers were ready to print the false story alleging that the boycott had ended. As soon as the MIA leadership found this out, they headed to bars to spread the word that the boycott had not ended. When the white groups realized that their tactics would not work, they resorted to violence. In fact, the houses of prominent black leaders were bombed, including that of Dr. King. Next, white groups turned to the law; that is, on February 21, they indicted 89 blacks with the charge that it was against the law to engage in a boycott. Dr. King was one of the 89 individuals indicted and he was ordered to pay $500 plus another $500 in court costs. If he failed to do this, he had the option of spending 386 days in the state penitentiary (Williams, 1987).

Efforts to End the Strike

White groups also tried to break down the "private taxi" system by enforcing laws that would not have otherwise been enforced. For instance, blacks were often given citations or even arrested for driving too slow in residential neighborhoods. In addition, some white groups tried to revoke liability insurance policies or not make these available to any member of the black community who was interested in driving through the city. So some found insurance brokers outside the city in order to obtain policies for their vehicles. The extraordinary response from the black community included "rolling churches." These churches were given this name due to the fact that they had purchased station wagons or other form of transportation in order to move their church members around the city. Despite the pressure to end the boycott, blacks were true to their objective and stayed off the buses.

In one incident, it is said that a white bus driver stopped to let off a lone black man in a predominantly black neighborhood. While the bus driver was looking through the rear view mirror he saw an old black woman rushing toward the bus. In turn, the bus driver opened the door and said, "You don't have to rush auntie, I'll wait for you." The woman replied, "In the first place, I ain't your auntie. In the second place, I ain't rushing to get on your bus. I am jus' trying to catch up with that nigger who just got off, so I can hit him with this here stick" (Cozzens, 1997).

Other attempts were made by other groups to try to bring an end to the boycott. The businesses in downtown Montgomery were deeply affected by the boycott as less blacks were likely to shop in downtown. Thus, they formed a group called the Men of Montgomery and under this name they attempted to negotiate with the boycotters in order to end the boycott. Despite several attempts, the negotiations failed and the boycott continued (Cozzens, 1997).

The Legal Battles

Despite these failing attempts to end the boycott, the battle really took place in the courts. In fact, blacks had already filed motions before federal court while attempting to declare segregation in buses and other public places unconstitutional (Lewis, 1964). They were aided by the *Brown* v. *Board of Education* decision, which was, at the time, only two years old. In this decision, the court had ruled that segregation in schools was unconstitutional. Thus, the point was made (by blacks) that the unconstitutionality of school segregation was also applicable to other public places, including the bus system. The fact that the case was brought before federal court was also reassuring as these courts were more likely to act in an objective manner regarding any case involving blacks. At the end of all motions filed, the federal court declared in a 2–1 decision that segregation in buses was unconstitutional (Cozzens, 1997). The only dissent came from a Southern judge. However, on November 13, 1956, the U.S. Supreme Court upheld the federal court ruling with regard to the boycott. The Montgomery bus boycott was officially over, and the efforts of Rosa Parks, Martin Luther King, and others resulted in victory for blacks (Weisbrot, 1990).

BEYOND THE STRIKE

Despite the Supreme Court opinion and the obvious victory for blacks, the troubles affecting the black community were not over. Blacks returned to the buses on December 21, 1956, which was over a year after the boycott had started (Cozzens, 1997). However, soon after their return, snipers began to fire at buses, forcing the city to suspend bus operations after 5 P.M. Another group began an all-white bus service, while others engaged in bombings. The homes of two black leaders, two Baptist churches, and the people's service station were bombed. As a result, seven white men were arrested for the bombings and five of them were indicted. Despite the indictments, all of the men walked out of the court without paying a fine or serving a day in prison. The Ku Klux Klan (KKK) also tried to scare blacks by intimidating them; however, some argued that the KKK seemed to have lost their ability to inflict fear among the black community. As reported by Dr. King, ". . . one cold night a small Negro boy was seen warming his hands at a burning cross." On January 10 and 11, 1957, ministers from the MIA joined others from around the South in the city of Atlanta, Georgia, to form the Southern Christian Leadership Conference (SCLC). They elected Dr. Martin Luther King, Jr., as president (Cozzens, 1997).

The SCLC went on to work in different areas of the South for many years. Their objective continued to be blacks' freedom and independence from oppression. Some may argue that the gains of the Montgomery Boycott were small when compared to others. However, as argued by Roberta Wright, the Montgomery Boycott "helped to launch a 10-year national struggle for freedom and justice, the Civil Rights Movement, that stimulated others to do the same at home and abroad" (Cozzens, 1997).

SIT-INS

Soon after the Montgomery Boycott, sit-ins began to emerge. It began when, on February 1, 1960, Joseph McNeil, Franklin McCain, David Richmond, and Ezell Blair, Jr., walked into an F.W. Woolworth Company store in Greensboro, North Carolina (Cozzens, 1997). They purchased some school supplies and then went to be served at the lunch counter, which was segregated. They knew this but wanted to challenge the issue since they felt they should be served as they were like any other customer. When service was denied, they decided to initiate a sit-in. At first, this had little effect on the campus or the local area. However, the next day other students joined the original group and it grew larger and larger. News regarding this traveled quickly and was reported across the United States, after which other students in other campuses began to engage in similar acts (Williams, 1987).

The basic plan of the sit-in was that a group of students would go to a lunch counter and ask to be served. If they were served they would move on to the next counter. However, if service was denied they would not move until they had been served. If the students happen to be arrested, as it was often the case, a new group of students would replace them the next day. It should be mentioned that the students remained nonviolent and respectful at all times. In Nashville, students had some "do's" and "don'ts" during sit-ins. For instance, they were instructed to ". . . show yourself friendly on the counter at all times. Do sit straight and always face the counter. Don't strike back, or curse back if attacked. Don't laugh out. Don't hold conversations. Don't block entrances" (Cozzens, 1997). In addition, the clothing worn by students who engaged in sit-ins was formal. In fact, witnesses described the contrast of black protestors, who wore suits and ties and read class-related material while they participated in the sit-in, to white students who often showed up to harass the protestors. They often wore informal attire and used profanity when confronting their black counterparts.

The sit-ins brought individual victories in places like Nashville, Tennessee, where after a protest and several sit-ins, lunch counters began to serve blacks. By August 1961, the sit-ins had attracted over 70,000 participants and generated over 3,000 arrests. They continued even after the passage of the Civil Rights Act of 1964, which declared segregation at lunch counters to be illegal. Many regarded the sit-ins as an important shifting point of the civil rights struggle. According to journalist Louis Lomax, "they were proof that the Negro leadership class, epitomized by the NAACP, was no longer the prime mover in the Negro's social revolt. The demonstrations have shifted the desegregation battles from the courtroom to the marketplace" (Cozzens, 1997). In fact, the sit-ins showed that nonviolent action by the youth was a useful weapon in the civil rights movement.

THE BLACK VOTE

Although the sit-ins had a significant impact on the civil rights movement, the fact remained that blacks continued to face other challenges. One of these was the fact that blacks were eligible to vote but it was often very difficult for them to become registered voters. When blacks attempted to register to vote they would find empty offices. When they met with the registrar's office personnel, blacks were told they had to take a test and upon successful completion of the test, they would receive their voter's registration card. It was often the case that the black applicant was better educated than the registrar. However, despite successful completion of the test, blacks were often told that they had failed and therefore their ability to vote had been denied until further notice.

In addition, attempts by blacks to become registered voters were met with resistance from whites. This often took place in Selma, Alabama—a small town of about 30,000 people. It was located in Dallas County, where only 1% of eligible blacks were registered to vote. On October 7, 1963, when blacks tried to organize a "Freedom Day," a local photographer, under orders from Sheriff Jim Clark, took pictures of the 250 blacks who lined up to register to vote (Williams, 1987). The photographer, upon approaching the blacks in line, asked them if they knew what their employers would think of them if they knew what they had done. Police personnel were readily available to beat those individuals who brought food or water to those in line to register to vote.

In addition, blacks were often attacked in Selma and surrounding cities as they attempted to launch protests for not being allowed to register to vote (Lewis, 1964). Prominent blacks were either beaten, arrested, or at times even killed. Jimmie Lee Jackson, a young Vietnam War veteran was killed in one of the protests as he tried to protect his mother from the abuses of police officers and others ready to subdue the black protestors. Out of a cry to march Jackson's body from Selma to the state capitol in Montgomery, the idea of a civil rights march emerged.

THE MARCH

The march started on Sunday, March 7, 1965 (Schneider and Schneider, 2001). As marchers crossed the Edmund Pettus Bridge in Selma, named after a confederate general, they were met by law enforcement officials, some of whom were on horseback. They had orders from Governor George Wallace to stop the march. The officers followed the governor's orders and instructed the marchers to disperse, or to go home or to church. They specifically affirmed that the march "will not continue." Almost immediately after making this announcement, the law enforcement officials confronted the marchers. They fired tear gas into the crowd and severely beat the marchers. Among the marchers, there were women, elderly couples, and children. The beating was induced without any regard for gender or age. That night, television stations interrupted their normal programming in order to show clips of the violence that had taken place in Selma. In that period, ABC was showing a documentary on Nazi war crimes, *Judgment at Nuremberg*. Many of the viewers watching the violence in Selma thought that this was part of the Nazi documentary. George B. Leonard recalled his feelings after seeing the clash between the police and the marchers:

> A shrill cry of terror, unlike any that had passed through a TV set, rose up as the troopers lumbered forward, stumbling sometimes on the fallen bodies. . . . Periodically the top of a helmeted head emerged from the cloud, followed by a club on the upswing. The club and

the head would disappear into the cloud of gas and another club would bob up and down. Unhuman. No other word can describe the motions. . . . My wife, sobbing, turned and walked away, sing, 'I can't look any more . . .' (Cozzens, 1997)

Dr. Martin Luther King, who had been preaching in Atlanta on "Bloody Sunday," as the day had been called, immediately began to make plans to conduct a new march on Tuesday. He called on people from all over the United States to join him in Selma. The response was energizing as hundreds of people, after being shocked by what they had seen on television, dropped everything they had been doing to join Dr. King in Selma (Williams, 1987).

THE SECOND MARCH IN SELMA

Prior to the second march in Selma, organizers tried to prevent any further violence by requesting a court order prohibiting the police from stopping the march. The federal judge who heard the petition had, in prior instances, sided with civil rights causes. However, this time, he expressed his desire to hold further hearings later on during the week. The judge issued a restraining order stating that the march could not take place until he considered the petition further. The march organizers had to make a tough decision. One the one hand, protesters had come from all over the United States to participate in the march and due to this the organizers felt an obligation to conduct the march. On the other hand, they did not want to disobey the judge's orders, particularly in that this judge was one of the few Southern judges who often sympathized with civil rights issues. Dr. King made the decision to hold a short march and then a prayer, and turn back around soon after crossing the bridge. Doing this would not violate the judge's orders to not hold the march from Selma to Montgomery, while at the same time it would also likely prevent Bloody Sunday taking place again.

King asked marchers who could stay to remain in Selma for another march. One of the individuals who decided to stay was James Reeb, a white minister from Boston. That night Reeb went out to dinner with some friends. After leaving the restaurant, being unfamiliar with Selma he took a wrong turn and ended up in a white neighborhood, where he was beaten with a club. He was taken to a hospital in Birmingham, but he died before arriving there. This event brought national attention, which angered many blacks as they pointed out that the death of Jimmie Lee Jackson had gone almost unnoticed but now the death of a white minister received national attention.

A week after Reeb's death, the federal judge declared that the state could not block the march. Subsequent to the ruling, President Johnson federalized the Alabama National Guard to provide protection to the marchers. Almost 20 days after Bloody Sunday, on March 21, the marchers crossed over the Edmond Pettus Bridge and continued on their march for five days. The march, unlike previous ones, did not attract any violence (Cozzens, 1997).

When the marchers entered Montgomery, they were 25,000 strong. Among the marchers were civil rights members with national distinction, such as Dr. Martin Luther

King, Rosa Parks, and John Lewis. The return to Montgomery, a city that had been at the center of the civil rights movement ten years earlier because of the Montgomery Bus Boycott, was a triumphant moment. Coretta Scott King, wife of Dr. Martin Luther King, remembered the arrival in Montgomery as follows:

> I kept thinking about ten years earlier, how we were . . . just blacks [in the movement] . . . [But the Selma to Montogomery march] had Catholic priests, and nuns, and you had other clergy, and you had a lot of White people. It was really a beautiful thing to pass Dexter Avenue Church [where King had preached while in Montgomery] and go toward the capitol marching together. (Cozzens, 1997)

The end of the march marked a victory for civil rights advocates but it also brought sadness to some close to Viola Liuzzo, a white homemaker from Detroit, who after participating in the march was shot and killed by Klansmen as she drove back to Selma from Montgomery. The fight for civil rights was far from over, but the march from Selma to Montgomery materialized the struggle for equality and made national news in the days and weeks after it ended. Specifically, the march sent the message that whereas ten years earlier blacks had timidly asked if they could sit in the front of the bus, now they were ready to demand, in a public forum, their rights as American citizens. In addition, the march sent the message to the rest of the country that the courts and the presidency were on the side of blacks and their struggle for equality. The momentum was there but the dangers associated with the struggle still remained in place (Williams, 1987).

THE NAACP

It is unthinkable that the civil rights movement would have triumphed without the assistance of certain organizations that supported the struggle for equal rights. One of these organizations was the National Association for the Advancement of Colored People (NAACP). On February 12, 1909, a group of blacks formed the NAACP in an attempt to answer "the call" to fight for equality of blacks in the United States (Schneider and Schneider, 2001). Some of the most notorious founders of the NAACP who answered "the call" included Ida Wells-Barnett, W. E. B. DuBois, Henry Mocowitz, Mary White Ovington, Oswald Garrison Villard, and William English Walling. In 1910, the NAACP took the national identity of an organization that fought legal battles for the advancement of blacks. Although the NAACP lost a few of its early cases, it committed its resources to fight all major civil rights cases that came up in the courts.

In 1913, as a direct response to President Woodrow Wilson's introduction of segregation in the federal government, the NAACP launched a protest. The NAACP received widespread recognition due to the protest, which led to an increase in its membership. It remained active as an organization fighting legal battles and protesting events or other forms of propaganda that aimed at continuing the oppression of blacks. The NAACP was a powerful force behind civil rights movements. In fact, the students who decided to conduct the sit-ins mentioned earlier were also supported by the NAACP (http://www.NAACP.org).

During the civil rights era, the NAACP was activated to rally support and enhance the presence of blacks in marches and allow for registration of black voters in the South. This organization remains active today in addressing the concerns of the black community. It is clear that the NAACP continues to fight for the rights of blacks in the United States. Restated, their goal and objective has continued to be equal rights even if the marches and boycotts have ceased to exist. The fight, according to members, is now more political and less visible. It calls for equality in pay and advancement of blacks in the community. It further calls for the fair treatment of blacks in the criminal justice system. Perhaps the most visible and contended interaction of blacks with the criminal justice system relates to law enforcement. That is, it relates to the manner in which blacks are treated by police officers in the course of a traffic stop or a similar instance. It is not surprising, then, to recognize that the NAACP is currently one of the most active civil rights organizations with regard to racial profiling.

The LULAC

One of the organizations that supported the civil rights movement and came to be known throughout the United States for their activism in promoting the rights of minorities was the League of United Latin American Citizens (LULAC). For over 75 years, LULAC has been recognized as the primary organization whose aim is to promote civil rights for minorities in general and Latinos specifically (http://www.LULAC.org). When the United States annexed a third of Mexico's territory after the Mexican War, nearly 77,000 Mexicans became U.S. citizens. For years to come after the annexation, these former Mexican nationals turned U.S. citizens became the subject of much discrimination and prejudice. In fact, signs that stated "No Mexicans Allowed" were often found in hotels, restaurants, and other public facilities. These signs depicted the attitude of most people in the United States at the time (http://www.LULAC.org). The racial bias and discriminatory practices toward Hispanics had escalated to such levels that members of the Hispanic community in Texas felt that the only solution to their troubles was to unite and create powerful organizations. Although several organizations were created, three came to the forefront of the civil rights struggle for Hispanics. These organizations included the Order of the Sons of America, with councils in Somerset, Pearsall, Corpus Christi, and San Antonio. The second was the Knights of America in San Antonio. And the third was the League of Latin American Citizens, with councils in Harlingen, Brownsville, Laredo, Penitas, La Grulla, McAllen, and Gulf.

On August 14, 1927, an attempt was made to consolidate all of the organizations under the umbrella of a major entity. Delegates from the Order of the Sons of America, the Knights of America, and other similar organizations traveled to Harlingen to attend the formal installation of the League of Latin American Citizens. The new organization, under the leadership of attorney Alonso S. Perales of Harlingen, was invited by the leadership of the Order of the Sons of America to unite with them as a first step toward the unification of all Mexican American organizations (Williams, 1987).

There were doubts about the merger since there were personal issues that had emerged among the leaders of the different Hispanic associations. However, the Order of the Sons of America and the Knights of America made an agreement to unite even if the League of Latin American Citizens did not agree on unifying. The unification did not happen at once. Instead, all organizations involved in the proposed merger waited for a year for the unification to take place, when delegates were elected and the earlier plans to unify were executed. The unified front carried the motto, "All for one and one for all," proposed by J.T. Canales. This was meant to serve as a constant reminder of the many challenges faced when proposing to unify while keeping in mind the interests of the majority.

The merger occurred after much planning and discussion. In fact, the committee that was ultimately responsible for conducting the merger considered the constitution of the new organization to be one of the most important tasks to accomplish. After much consideration, the committee decided to merge the best aspects of the constitutions of all three organizations—Order of the Sons of America, the Knights of America, and the League of Latin American Citizens. Once this was done, the next step was to come up with a name that would also give recognition to the three merging organizations and its membership. Again, after much debate and discussion, it was decided that the name of the newest but fastest growing organization, the League of Latin American Citizens, would be modified and preserved when naming the new organization. Thus, the League of United Latin American Citizens (LULAC) came to existence on February 17, 1929. The delegates who had proposed and approved the merger were very pleased with the leadership of Ben Garza, one of the League's members, that it was almost unanimously proposed that he become the first president of LULAC. The delegates also agreed to hold the first LULAC convention on May 19, 1929, in Corpus Christi, Texas (http://www.LULAC.org).

Throughout the years, the LULAC came to be known as an organization that represented and defended the rights of Hispanics in the United States. Specifically, the LULAC has been very active in fighting legal battles in the courts in order to desegregate schools in Texas and other states (1930); pressuring the U.S. Census Bureau to reclassify persons of Mexican descent from "Mexican" to "white" (1936); advocating for equal salaries for Hispanics (1966); creating the Mexican American Legal Defense and Education Fund (MALDEF), which has become the legal arm of the Hispanic community; and addressing issues of concern to the Hispanic community, such as racial profiling (http://www.LULAC.org).

THE ACLU

Another major organization concerned with, for the most part, the civil rights of citizens is the American Civil Liberties Union (ACLU). The history of the ACLU dates back to 1920, when Crystal Eastman and Roger Baldwin founded the organization (Walker, 1990). The organization was originally called the Civil Liberties Bureau. Eastman studied law at New York University after receiving her undergraduate degree at Vassar. She married twice and was the mother of two children. Eastman was instrumental in passing workers' compensation laws and conducted extensive research into industrial accidents. She was also a women's suffrage activist who managed the Wisconsin Women's Suffrage Campaign in 1912. She assisted in the creation of the Congressional Union, while leading the New York branch of the Women's Peace Party, which opposed World War I. In the words of the *Nation*, Eastman was "for thousands a symbol of what the free woman might be" (Walker, 1990).

Roger Baldwin, the cofounder of the ACLU, graduated from Harvard University with his bachelor's degree in 1904 and his master's in 1905. He taught sociology, worked as a probation officer, and served as secretary of the Civil League of St. Louis prior to heading the American Union against Militarism, a predecessor of the ACLU. This particular organization represented and defended conscientious objectors and draft resisters during World War I. In 1918, Baldwin served nine months in prison for resisting the draft. After being released, he joined the Industrial Workers of the World (IWW). All of these efforts led to his service as the first director and then national chairman of the ACLU.

Although some argue that the ACLU was founded with noble intentions, reports at the time of its creation related ties with the communist party/ideology. In 1931, the Special House Committee to Investigate Communist Activities stated that

> The American Civil Liberties Union is closely affiliated with the community movement in the United States, and fully 90 percent of its efforts are on behalf of communists who have come into conflict with the law. It claims to stand for free speech, free press and free assembly, but it is quite apparent that the main function of the ACLU is an attempt to protect the communists." (U.S. Congress Archives, 1931)

Despite charges of communist affiliation, the ACLU won a great deal of legal battles advocating civil liberties. For instance, it won free speech cases, including the right of a group of Jehovah's Witnesses to enjoy freedom of the press, which had been denied to them due to a Georgia statute requiring a permit in order to distribute any literature. Other cases included the "monkey trial" of John Scopes in 1925, which allowed the teaching of evolution in schools. In addition, it succeeded in lifting the ban on James Joyce's *Ulysses.* Also, it won the case involving Henry Ford where his right to distribute antiunion materials was successfully defended.

Other cases that were represented and won by the ACLU throughout the United States included discrimination cases and those related to forcing children to salute the U.S. flag, voting rights of blacks in Texas, and censorship of popular literature including films. Clearly, the ACLU has gained the respect of civil libertarians, while it has been deemed by some, mostly conservatives, as an organization which aims at ruining the foundation of the United States. Regardless of which point of view is correct, it is clear that the ACLU has been and continues to play an active role in the defense of civil rights and liberties in the United States. In 1999, the ACLU made national headlines with the publication *Driving While Black: Racial Profiling in Our Nation's Highways.* This publication narrated incidents where motorists were allegedly stopped due to their minority status and not a traffic-related reason. The publication gave rise to a national debate on racial profiling.

SUMMARY

Most discussions centered on racial profiling fail to acknowledge that this particular issue would not be in existence today unless some members of the minority community felt marginalized and exploited. Restated, unless we trace back the roots of marginalization and exploitation, we cannot fully comprehend the different dimensions of racial profiling. Thus, in this chapter, I have tried to present a brief historical account of slavery and the civil rights movement as it relates to the exploitation of African Americans and their struggle to achieve equality. Throughout the civil rights struggle, the role that organizations such as the NAACP, LULAC, and the ACLU played has been remarkable. In sum, it is clear, after reviewing the period of slavery leading to the struggle for civil rights as introduced in this chapter, that

a. The exploitation of African Americans in the United States was deeply rooted in violence.
b. The struggle for equality took many forms, including boycotts, marches, and an Underground Railroad.
c. The United States was geographically divided with respect to slavery and the freedom of African Americans.
d. The role of organizations such as the NAACP, LULAC, and the ACLU was crucial to the civil rights movement.

Given this, it should not come as a surprise that some members of the minority community today still feel suspicious of the actions of the law enforcement community involving them. Specifically, some cite the apparent overrepresentation of minorities among people who appear in court and in correctional systems as evidence that racism remains a problem in the United States. As you may have guessed, the law enforcement community has not escaped these criticisms. In fact, citing statistics which show a large number of minority drivers stopped and searched, members of civil rights organizations argue that racism is currently taking place in America's highways. They argue that some police officers specifically target minority drivers by stopping them for alleged traffic infractions and performing searches without probable cause. It is argued that racial profiling is taking place and that it serves as an institutional means to manipulate, harass, and in most cases, control members of the minority community. Regardless of how you may feel about these claims, it is clear that given the history of slavery and the civil rights movement, the United States serves as an ideal platform in which to launch these accusations and find support.

It is still the case that thousands of Americans believe that the civil rights struggle has not ended. In fact, it is widely held, particularly among minorities, that racism still continues today, although it is more secretive and less visible when compared to the civil rights era. Organizations that were popular during the civil rights movement (i.e., NAACP, LULAC, and ACLU) have found a new role in the current struggle for equality. In a more organized and unified form, they have launched campaigns to end discrimination in the criminal justice system generally and in law enforcement specifically. Their campaigns have been launched in the courts and in public forums, where issues such as racial profiling are being discussed with members of the community in an effort to increase citizenry awareness. Some claim that highlighting such issues within the context of the civil rights struggle of the previous era is nothing more than a publicity campaign by the civil rights organizations in an effort to remain legitimate. Others, however, claim that today more than ever in the history of the United States, the role of the civil rights groups is crucial to the preservation of individual rights. Regardless of which side is correct, it remains a fact that racial profiling has surged as a pressing issue which must be discussed and examined further by all members of the community.

References

Blockson, Charles (1984). "Escape from Slavery: The Underground Railroad." *National Geographic Magazine*. Vol. 166, No. 1, pp. 3–39.

Columbia Electronic Encyclopedia (2006). 6th ed. Columbia University Press.

Cozzens, Lisa (1997). "Birmingham." http://www.watson.org/~lisa/blackhistory/civilrights-55-65/selma.html

Cozzens, Lisa (1997). "Freedom Rides." http://www.watson.org/~lisa/blackhistory/civilrightws-55-65/freeride.html

Cozzens, Lisa (1997). "March on Washington." http://www.watson.org/~lisa/blackhistory/civilrights-55-65/marchwas.html

Cozzens, Lisa (1997). "Mississippi and Freedom Summer." http://www.watson.org/~lisa/blackhistory/civilrights-55-65/missippi.html

Cozzens, Lisa (1997). "Montgomery Bus Boycott." http://www.watson.org/~lisa/blackhistory/civilrights-55-65/monthbus.html

Cozzens, Lisa (1997). "Sit-Ins." http://www.watson.org/~lisa/blackhistory/civilrights-55-65/sit-ins. html

Huggins, Nathan Irvin (1980). *Slave and Citizen: The Life of Frederick Douglass*. Boston: Little, Brown. http://www.LULAC.org http://www.NAACP.org

Lewis, Anthony (1964). *Portrait of a Decade: The Second American Revolution*. New York: Random House, p. 86.

Mellon, James (1988). *Bullwhip Davis: The Slaves Remember*. New York: Grove Press Books.

Schneider, Dorothy and Schneider, Carl J. (2001). *An Eyewitness History of Slavery in America: From Colonial Times to the Civil War*. New York: Checkmark Books.

Smedley, R.C. (1883). *History of Underground Railroad in Chester and the Neighboring Counties of Pennsylvania*. Lancaster, PA: Office of the Journal.

Thomas, Sandra (2006). *A Biography of the Life of Frederick Douglass*. Rochester.

U.S. Congress Archives (1931). *Special House Committee to Investigate Communist Activities*. Washington, DC: U.S. Government Printing Office

Walker, Samuel (1990). *In Defense of American Liberties: A History of the ACLU*. Carbondale, IL: Southern Illinois University Press.

Weisbrot, Robert (1990). *Freedom Bound: A History of America's Civil Rights Movement*. New York: W.W. Norton & Company, pp. 28–29.

Williams, Juan (1987). *Eyes on the Prize: America's Civil Rights Years, 1954–1965*. New York: Viking Penguin Inc., p. 62.

CHAPTER 5

Critical Issues in Racial Profiling

Racial profiling continues to be one of the most frequently debated topics in our society today. Newspapers and other news sources periodically report alleged tendencies of police departments to engage in racial profiling practices. Further, these same media often publish quotes or editorial articles written by civil rights activists who claim that they "are not surprised by the racial profiling numbers of police departments" as they have "always known that this problem exists in the law enforcement community." Sadly, the often-misinformed public formulates its opinion from these rather superficial news stories that seldom discuss the complexity of the racial profiling issue.

Traditionally, when the public experiences difficulty in understanding certain scientific concepts, academics have gained a reputation for being called in to better understand and explain the unknown or unfamiliar, using their ability to separate myths from fact in an attempt to derive the "truth." However, in the case of racial profiling, for reasons beyond the scope of this book, this does not seem to have taken place. In fact, it is argued that as most academics who have conducted research on racial profiling have failed to address the critical factors affecting the issue, the public are confused about the issue. This has led to the daring position that most of us have taken regarding racial profiling; that is, it exists across the board but we are not exactly sure if the measures currently in place to determine this support our position. I regard this as a "daring" position since it is not well established by academic research and seems to suffer from a particular absence of rationality and maturity.

However, at the end of the day, we find ourselves with studies after studies (Leung et al., 2005; Schafer and Mastrofski, 2005; Petrocelli, Piquero, and Smith, 2003; Smith and Alpert, 2002) that claim, collectively or individually, to have unique insights into the racial profiling paradox. Unfortunately, most of these studies (Lee, 2005; Illya, 2006; Lang, Johnson and Voas, 2005; Skogan and Meares, 2004; Hart et al., 2003), although interesting to read, don't answer the common question posed by thousands of chiefs of police and police professionals regarding racial profiling. That is, how can a chief of police or law enforcement administrator know that racial profiling is a problem in his/her police department? How can they measure this phenomenon?

Although researchers claim to know the answer to this question, they often point to the relevant "data" as the source of insights regarding this issue. Sadly, most people who may be easily impressed with an advanced statistical analysis performed on police contact data may quickly accept the "findings" of a study as the "answer to racial profiling measures." However, in doing so, they lose focus of the important point: Can data answer the question of whether or not racial profiling is taking place? In my opinion, it cannot. I will outline the reasons supporting my position and will also provide a sense of what factors, in my view, we should consider when attempting to determine if racial profiling is taking place in a particular location.

THE COLLECTION OF DATA

In order to better understand the reasons why data may not hold the ultimate answer to the racial profiling problem, we should first explore how data is collected and recorded in police departments across the United States. It is difficult to generalize the data collection methods used by different police agencies in that these vary in size, budget, organizational structure, and level of complexity. Despite this, most police agencies, regardless of their size, typically designate an employee to gather the data and structure it in a specific manner for the command staff to review. Oftentimes, in rural settings, this person may also be the chief of police or someone who also has other administrative duties. Moreover, officers who were injured on the job and cannot return to patrol duties right away are often assigned to what they describe as the "wonderful task" of gathering and analyzing data. However, in large police departments, who often enjoy the support of civilian personnel, chiefs of police designate an entire unit to crime analysis, including, but not exclusive of, the collection and analysis of racial profiling data.

Although most police officers will quickly show you the many plaques and certificates occupying their office walls, which suggest the vast amount of training they received, very few of these, if any, are related to the analysis of data. As you would expect, most of these plaques and certificates relate to trainings in areas involving the identification, apprehension, and interrogation of suspects. Seldom do we find police departments with personnel trained in areas related to the analysis and interpretation of data. Despite the fact that institutions don't often prioritize or value—or, in some cases, are not able to afford—training on data analysis for their personnel, the number of personnel who do not understand data analysis is slowly decreasing. That is, in recent years, there has been a surge in police personnel (civilian and commissioned officers) who are seeking graduate degrees from academic institutions throughout the United States. The availability of online programs has made this task easier for them. Despite this, it will be some time before most police institutions benefit from the data analysis expertise acquired by officers enrolled in graduate degree programs. In the meantime, most police organizations are ill-prepared to analyze data related to racial profiling, which is likely to affect the community's perception of police work.

DATA ACCURACY

The accuracy of data collected is subject to reporting and recording errors (Maxfield and Babbie, 2005). In fact, the general rule in research is that the lesser the number people who handle the data, the greater the possibility that the data will not be corrupted. Restated, the data may not be accurate if more than enough people handle it before reaching its final destination. In most cases, racial profiling data, otherwise known as traffic-stop data, originates from the traffic officer who makes the initial contact with the suspect. Just imagine how accurate this data may be as we leave it up to most police officers to determine, single-handedly, the race or ethnicity of the person when recording the data. If you think this is a rather easy task, think again.

Oftentimes, these officers face individuals who may be Caucasian but married to a person of Hispanic descent and therefore carry a Spanish surname. What ethnicity or race does this person represent? Is she Caucasian or Hispanic? In other instances, officers are asked to make this racial/ethnic distinction on individuals who may represent two or three different races or ethnicities. For instance, a person whose mother was Caucasian but whose father was Hispanic would make this person a "White Hispanic." Sadly, in most states gathering data on racial profiling requires that the officer make a distinction between the two. In other words, is the person White or Hispanic? Although it is widespread knowledge that race is not the same as ethnicity and therefore one could accurately be regarded as a White Hispanic without the suggestion of contradicting terms, the law enforcement community, for the most part, does not enjoy the benefit of combining race and ethnicity into a single category. Thus, officers are required to make the distinction and separate these two categories. As you can imagine, this leads to interesting conversations regarding the alleged "intent" of officers when they record the racial/ethnic category of a driver. In other words, if the driver was a Hispanic female whose last name was "Smith" but the officer recorded her race/ethnicity as "White," then clearly the officer had the intent of lying. Not necessarily. That is, perhaps the officer felt that she seemed to have Caucasian-like features that outweigh the suggestion that she was in fact Hispanic, which was inferred by her Spanish last name.

In other cases, where the officer is mandated to be guided by the race/ethnicity of the individual as reported by the Department of Public Safety or the information presented in the individual's driver's license, there is very little discretion exercised by the officer. It should also be noted that most Departments of Public Safety, which make this information available to the officer via a computer, do not record ethnicity; thus, officers have to record the prescribed race of the person even if the last name and other physical indicators of the individual suggest otherwise. None of these possibilities rule out the fact that in some cases, officers may in fact purposely disregard the ethnicity or race of the individual in an attempt to sabotage the system, or they may simply disregard the importance of reporting accurate traffic-stop data.

MECHANISMS OF DATA COLLECTION

Once the traffic-stop data is reported by the patrol officer, it typically reaches a central repository which often resides in the communications/dispatch department. In rural agencies, the equivalent of the central repository is the chief of police or a member of the small command staff whose responsibilities are to oversee the data reporting mechanisms. In larger settings, the repository is either an electronic data component or a physical location where all paper copies of citations or contact cards (citation-like forms which enhance the efficiency of traffic data collection mechanisms) are filed. Regardless of the setting, the documents where the traffic data is recorded are subsequently transcribed to a computer program, which allows police departments to produce spreadsheets or other required reports. The electronic mechanisms often include scantron machines so that officers can feed information on traffic-related contacts to scantron cards during their particular shift. These scantron cards are considered to be better options to retain accurate data as they eliminate the possible errors made by clerks, who enter hundreds if not thousands of citations issued in a given day, thus running the high risk of entering erroneous information.

As explained earlier, although the handling of data varies from one department to the other, it is subject to the interpretation (early on) of a police officer and then of a person in charge of collecting and recording the data for a particular agency. Once the data reaches the individual responsible for the collection of data for the entire department, depending on the level of sophistication of the department, the data is kept in the original traffic citations (in small departments) or is entered into a sophisticated software system with the intent of producing printouts showing totals relevant to traffic contacts at a given time. The latter is typically the case with mid-size to larger police agencies.

Most police departments, regardless of their size, seem to have the ability of recording, collecting, and reporting traffic-stop data. However, they face challenges while interpreting the data they collect. Data analysis also seems to have political and social implications for the departments, the residents of a community, and the country as a whole.

When considering the utility of traffic-stop data, we must stop and reflect on the data we are considering. That is, traffic-stop data typically represents a police officer's contact with the community in the course of a traffic stop. Particularly, the information captured in a traffic contact typically includes the individual's race, gender, driver's license number, current address, location where citation was issued, nature of citation, whether or not a search was conducted, and whether an arrest was made as a result of the traffic contact. Although some believe that this information is useful in determining if a police officer is racially profiling, I would argue otherwise. Specifically, I would argue that we have no way of determining, by virtue of the limited information contained in a traffic citation, whether or not an officer intended to issue a citation based on the suspect's racial or ethnic background. You consider racial profiling for what it is—the action by an officer to issue a citation or perform a search on a suspect due to the fact that the person, although not suspicious or guilty of a criminal act, is of a race or ethnicity not well received by the officer. Given this, how could we possibly determine an officer's intent or racist tendencies based on traffic-stop data? Some may argue that if the officer's citations seem to overrepresent minority drivers, the officer "must" be guilty of racial profiling. I would argue that this is not necessarily the case as some officers may be assigned to predominantly minority areas of town where most of the citations they will issue, regardless of any bias, will likely be toward minority drivers. Moreover, officers are accused of racially profiling if their citations seem to have a higher number or percentage of minority motorists than those that reside in the town or city. For instance, if 200 citations are issued to blacks in a given month but the particular community where this took place only has 120 black residents, it is almost certain, in the view of some, that the officer must be racist. I would argue, again, that this is not necessarily the case as some of these citations may have been issued in highways or interstates to individuals who do not reside in the city/town. The point is that although there is a possibility that the disproportionate issuance of citations to minorities may be a "sign" of racial profiling, it may also be a result of traffic enforcement in settings where minorities seem to prevail when compared to the rest of the area. The bottom line is that we should not conclude one point over the other given the limitations in the recording, reporting, and nature of traffic-stop data. Doing so, regardless of the viewpoint or conclusions drawn, would be unfair to the community specifically and police departments across the United States, generally.

BASELINES

An additional challenge presented by the traffic-contact data relates to the baseline for comparison. That is, assuming that the traffic-contact data will shed light on racial profiling practices, we would need to compare this data to a particular baseline to determine an officer's true intent. Although the options for the baseline vary from state to state, the norm seems to be the U.S. census data. The rationale of using this data is that comparing the number of individuals stopped in the course of a traffic stop to the number of persons living in a particular community would reveal if officers are disproportionately stopping minorities. The problem of using this particular data source is that census data, as we have discovered in the past two censuses, is not accurate and often underrepresents individuals belonging to a certain socioeconomic status or racial/ethnic backgrounds. In addition, the census data takes account of only those people who agreed to participate in the census survey. That is, it excludes individuals who may not wish to participate. This is further complicated by the fact that the census is conducted every ten years, which makes it rather difficult for a researcher to regard this data as accurate, particularly as we reach the ninth year after the last census was conducted. The fact that the information may be dated is particularly relevant in communities which grow at steady rates and therefore change demographics rather quickly. Another point to be made about the census relates to the notion that it reports on individuals who reside in a particular community and does not take into account the individuals who may drive through a particular area of town on a daily basis. However, in some communities, most citations issued in the course of a traffic stop are given to individuals who do not reside in that particular community. This renders census data as "useless" in the overall analysis of traffic-stop data for studying racial profiling.

I have often wondered why some are eager to use the U.S. census data as a baseline when comparing traffic-stop data? Perhaps it is our tendency to come up with "quick fixes" to complex problems such as those related to racial profiling. Perhaps the most tragic aspect of this particular baseline does not relate to its limitations but rather to the fact that many in the media and related groups are quick to use and make reference to the census data when comparing it to traffic-stop data. This has a tendency of misinforming the public and leading some to erroneously conclude that racial profiling is in fact taking place.

Some states have considered using driver's license data, which is typically collected by the Department of Public Safety (DPS) or otherwise known as the Department of Motor Vehicles (DMV). They collect this data from drivers at the time they register to receive a driver's license. Some of the information collected includes the driver's self-proclaimed race or ethnicity, physical characteristics such as height and weight, and related demographical variables. Some claim that this particular data is ideal when analyzing racial profiling data since, after all, in the case of DPS/DMV data, the information contained derives from the driving population and is not collected every ten years as in the case of the U.S. census. However, in some states (as in Texas) the DPS/DMV collect information only on the race of the driver, thus regarding Hispanics as either whites or blacks. Thus, comparing this data and traffic-stop data, which takes ethnicity into account, might mislead the public. In addition, this particular data source is area specific; thus, researchers can only obtain this data based on zip codes, area codes, or city limits. This, limits its comparison to traffic stop data, which often includes out-of-town drivers with a data set limited to city/area residents.

In recent years, some have proclaimed that the Fair Roads Standard, which derives from the U.S. census, is the most useful tool when analyzing racial profiling. The Fair Roads Standard measures the number of households in a given community which have access to vehicles. Specifically, this information is derived from the U.S. census; one of the questions in the census aims at recording the head of household's race/ethnicity while asking if this person has access to at least one vehicle. Although superficially this baseline may be sufficient to some, it is in fact flawed when applied to racial profiling data. That is, the Fair Roads Standard only considers the race/ethnicity of the head of household, which excludes individuals who may be of a different race/ethnicity but may live in the same household. Further, it fails to record the number and race of other drivers of the same household, thus failing to count the number of individuals who may encounter a police officer in the course of a traffic stop. Further, like its counterparts (census and DPS/DMV), it is specific only to a community, thus excluding the high volume of nonresident contacts made by officers in the course of traffic stops. As is clear, none of these baseline options are ideal when analyzing racial profiling data. Unfortunately, the public media outlets don't seem to care one way or another about educating themselves or those they serve regarding the complexities and limitations presented by these baselines. Instead, they choose to use these baselines, without much regard for accuracy and relevance, when analyzing racial profiling data. This results in definitive statements about police departments with regard to "racial profiling" tendencies, which the public seems eager and ready to accept without questioning the process that led those making the statements to attain these conclusions.

SEARCHES

Some claim that given the limited utility of traffic-contact data (as outlined earlier), we should focus on searches conducted in the course of a traffic stop. The argument is that search data do not pose the same limitations as traffic contacts. That is, search data do not require to be compared with a particular baseline—most of which pose limitations (as discussed earlier). Search data analysis involves the collection of the total number of searches of Caucasian motorists. This serves as a baseline or departure point when analyzing the searches of members of minority groups. When reporting on these searches, researchers make statements such as, "in this particular city/town, Blacks were 3 times more likely (than whites) to be searched." Thus it facilitates the comparison of minority searches to Caucasian searches with the intent of obtaining a ratio for all minority searches.

Further analysis on search data is conducted by examining the "success" ratio of all searches—that is, whether or not the searches conducted resulted in contraband being seized—particularly those of minority drivers. Once the "success" rate of searches is obtained, minority search success rates are compared to those of their Caucasian counterparts. This allows some to make statements such as "Hispanic searches produced contraband only 10% of the time, while Caucasian searches produced contraband almost 30% of the time." The argument introduced here is that although minorities have a higher probability of being searched than Caucasians, their searches do not produce as much contraband as searches performed on Caucasian drivers. Restated, the argument suggests that minorities were likely searched for reasons other than criminal suspicion (i.e., racism) since the end result of the search was not the discovery of criminality. It should be noted that in some instances, some researchers include, in their analysis of search data, information relevant to arrests. The arrest data is used by researchers to solidify the argument that minorities' arrests, like searches, are conducted disproportionately despite the fact that contraband is found at a lesser rate than in Caucasian searches.

The utility of search data with regard to racial profiling has been questioned by some researchers. They argue that no one can determine if a police department is engaging in racial profiling by relying on the apparently disproportionate number of searches on minorities. Further, it is argued that the notion that a police department is racist is not necessarily strengthened by the presence of a high number of arrests on minority drivers. These researchers argue that it is not possible to determine if the individual being searched really deserves to be searched. It is further argued that arrests produced as a result of a traffic stop and search are not necessarily related to the contraband seized as a result of a search. In other words, the driver could be arrested for an outstanding warrant which may not be necessarily related to a search that may have been conducted during the course of a traffic stop. Once again, we find that the utility of search and arrest data, similar to traffic contact data, is inconclusive.

ANALYZING DATA

Although there seems to be a great deal of debate as to the manner in which data should be analyzed, most of the individuals involved in it fail to recognize the following:

1. Racial profiling is, for the most part, an individual-based act and not one typically performed by an institution. The opposite would suggest that most officers in police departments across the United States regularly perform racist traffic stops. It should be noted, when considering this position, that racism at one time in history was institutionalized in some organizations, including some police departments. However, this is, for the most part, no longer the case.

2. Aggregate data on traffic stops performed by a group of individuals has a limited utility when diagnosing individual-based behavior.

3. Data on contacts, searches, and arrests made in the course of a traffic stop do not necessarily illustrate an individual officer's predisposition to stop a motorist based on his/her ethnicity or race.

4. Making definitive statements about racial profiling based on aggregate traffic-stop data for a particular organization tends to generalize the issue of racism while hiding individuals with racist tendencies who may serve in a particular police department.

IDENTIFYING RACIAL PROFILING

It is clear from the arguments presented earlier in this chapter that racial profiling measures are flawed and have a limited utility when determining if racial profiling in fact exists. I am sure that after reading the different issues that affect the validity and utility of traffic-stop data, you may be wondering if there is a correct way of measuring racial profiling in law enforcement. Although this book does not claim to present all the answers on racial profiling, it hopes to prompt the reader to think beyond the scope of the current approach and state of knowledge with regard to this issue. In so doing, you should remember that racial profiling being an individual-based problem must be measured at the individual level. That is, actions of individual officers should be reviewed in "real time" in order to constantly assess his/her behavior, particularly as it relates to racism. Some of the categories of information on individual officers that should be recorded and analyzed include, but are not limited to, the following:

1. Traffic-contact data while controlling for geographic location where the officer is assigned and the shift in which the officer operates. This is based on the fact that police officers assigned to predominantly minority areas of a locale may end up

coming in contact with minority motorists disproportionately when compared to Caucasians. Further, it is also a fact that officers assigned to day shift may have a different volume of contacts with minorities than officers who are not assigned to day shift.

2. Number and nature of complaints filed by citizens. It is often the case that police officers who are known to engage in racial profiling are also subject to unusually large numbers of complaints by citizens. The complaints do not have to specifically focus on racial profiling. They could include items such as the use of inappropriate language, disrespectfulness towards fellow officers, and engaging in unethical behavior.

3. Instances of excessive use of force. That is, the officer is often the subject of complaints on apparent instances where he/she displayed an unusual amount of force against subjects. While comparing to other officers and to Caucasian motorists, the officer in question would have used force disproportionately against minority motorists.

4. A review of the officer's search data reveals that the officer in question seems to search minorities disproportionately when compared to Caucasians. Further, most of the searches on minorities don't seem to result in contraband being seized. Whereas most or at least a large volume of searches on Caucasians seem to result in contraband being seized.

5. Officer makes racial comments while he/she is in the company of other officers. Further, the officer seems to have a particular disregard and hatred toward minorities.

6. Systematic review of video footages of officer–minority citizen interactions reveals the presence of comments which are negative or racist in nature.

These items are not meant to be definitive in nature. That is, they are only meant to serve as "signs" that may reveal if a particular officer is engaging in racial profiling. It is important to keep in mind that the presence or absence of several of these issues does not definitively point at racial profiling one way or another. However, it is likely that if an officer is experiencing most of the items referred to earlier, that particular officer is suspect of engaging in racial profiling.

Some police departments have purchased expensive software packages that are able to track some of these categories in an attempt to identify, early on, if the officer may be experiencing problems that may lead to racial profiling practices. The "Early Warning System" (EWS) has turned out to be a very useful tool in the early identification of "patterns" among individual officers that seem to suggest that the officer may have racial profiling tendencies or may be engaging in racial profiling practices. Most mid- to large-size police departments have been able to purchase and implement these systems in their organizations. Some departments are housing these systems in their Internal Affairs units so that officers can be subject to direct oversight by internal affairs personnel, whose responsibility is to hold accountable all officers to ethical and legal standards. However, smaller police departments are typically not able to afford the acquisition of these systems, which prohibits them from being able to systematically track their respective officers. Perhaps the most significant advantage of the EWS is that it allows for police supervisors to identify and intervene, oftentimes, before the racial profiling act has occurred. This system collects all pertinent data on police officers (i.e., number and nature of use of force incidents and complaints filed against an officer) and when the number of these incidents reaches a prescribed threshold, it alerts the operator, who in turn informs a police supervisor of the finding. The idea is that the officer who has been "flagged" by the system will be interviewed by a supervisor and the proper corrective action will be initiated. This is often the case where federal funding has become available for smaller agencies who could not otherwise afford the acquisition and implementation of the EWS.

SUMMARY

It is clear that there is no easy solution to the complexities affecting the racial profiling debate. After reading this chapter, I hope that you have attained a better understanding of the errors and omissions often incurred by researchers, political activists, and politicians when considering the most effective manner in which to measure racial profiling among police agencies. As I mentioned earlier, racial profiling is for the most part an individual-based phenomenon and not an institutional one. Thus, it requires the careful review of very specific information regarding an officer's daily interactions with all citizens, particularly with minorities.

Hopefully the frequently cited phrase—"education is power"—will apply to the racial profiling debate so that media outlets and all others in the public forum will cease to make definitive statements on whether or not a police department is racially profiling based on information that is not properly gathered or reported. Further, it is my hope that informed readers will begin to start questioning generalizations with respect to police departments derived from limited aggregate data, which may not be the most accurate source of information on racial profiling practices.

References

Hart, Jessica L., Larsen, Anne Marie, Litton, K. Shay, and Sullivan, Laura J. (2003). "Racial Profiling: At What Price?" *Journal of Forensic Psychology Practice.* Vol. 3, No. 2, pp. 72–88.

Illya, Lichtenberg (2006). "Driving While Black (DWB): Examining Race as a Tool in the War on Drugs." *Police Practice and Research.* Vol. 7, No. 1, March 2006, pp. 49–60.

Lang, James E., Johnson, Mark B., and Voas, Robert B. (2005). "Testing the Racial Profiling Hypothesis for Seemingly Disparate Traffic Stops on the New Jersey Turnpike." *Justice Quarterly.* Vol. 22, No. 2, June 2005, pp. 193–223.

Lee, Pao (2005)."An Analysis of Racial Profiling in La Crosse: Considering Subculture and the Context of Race Relations." Conference Paper—American Sociological Association. Annual Meeting 2005. Philadelphia, pp. 1–20.

Leung, Ambrose, Woolley, Frances, Tremblay, Richard E., and Vitaro, Frank (2005). "Who Gets Caught? Statistical Discrimination in Law Enforcement." *Journal of Socio-Economics*. Vol. 34, No. 3, May 2005, pp. 289–309.

Maxfield, Michael G. and Babbie, Earl R. (2005). *Research Methods for Criminal Justice and Criminology* (4th ed.). Belmont, CA: Wadsworth.

Petrocelli, Matthew, Piquero, Alex R., and Smith, Michael R. (2003). "Conflict Theory and Racial Profiling: An Empirical Analysis of Police Traffic Stop Data." *Journal of Criminal Justice*. Vol. 31, No. 1, January 2003, p. 1.

Schafer, Joseph A. and Mastrofski, Stephen D. (2005). "Police Leniency in Traffic Enforcement Encounters: Exploratory Findings from Observations and Interviews." *Journal of Criminal Justice*. Vol. 33, No. 3, May/June 2005, pp. 225–238.

Skogan, Wesley G. and Meares, Tracey L. (2004). "Lawful Policing." *Annals of the American Academy of Political and Social Science*. Vol. 593, May 2004, pp. 66–83.

Smith, Michael R. and Alpert, Geoffrey (2002). "Searching for Direction: Courts, Social Science, and the Adjudication of Racial Profiling Claims." *Justice Quarterly*. Vol. 19, No. 4, December 2002, p. 673.

CHAPTER 6

The Texas Experience

This chapter will focus on the history, requirements, political implications, and predicaments of Texas Senate Bill 1074, otherwise known as the Texas Racial Profiling Law. Highlighting the experience of Texas regarding its racial profiling law is not to suggest that this is the only state in the United States where such a law has been implemented. Rather, Texas is being focused on to simply tell the story about how one state was impacted by the legislative mandate that requires the collection, analysis, and reporting of traffic-stop data by law enforcement officials on an annual basis. The story of Texas' Racial Profiling Law represents the experiences of other states that, in the same way as Texas, have been subject to the passing of legislation intended to require law enforcement officials to collect and report racial profiling data. However, this story is unique in the sense that Texas has been the subject of national attention in cases involving racial discrimination and violence, such as the death of James Byrd on a Jasper road in 1998 (King, 2002) and the arrests of half of the African American population in Tulia in alleged drug raids which later proved to be flawed and biased (Nate, 2005).

It is clear that, years prior to the enactment of the racial profiling law in Texas, there were attempts made by a member of the state house, Representative Senfronia Thompson (Democrat from Houston), to introduce legislation relevant to racial profiling. Representative Thompson's proposed legislation moved through the hearing process but never made it for a general vote before the entire legislative body (Watson, 2006). Although some may claim that her attempts did not result in the passing of the law, they seemed to have prompted some legislators to focus on racial profiling. One of these legislators was state senator Royce West. Some have regarded West's role as crucial to the passing of Texas Senate Bill 1074. Senator West, a Democrat representing Dallas, authored the first draft of the bill; it was also influenced by civil rights activists across the state of Texas. Once the first draft of the bill was released, police organizations, chiefs of the six major cities in Texas (Dallas, Fort Worth, El Paso, Houston, San Antonio, and

Austin), and other law enforcement executives were invited to offer feedback on the provisions contained in the bill. It was clear that the law enforcement community and the civil rights groups were far from agreeing on the requirements that should be imposed on the law enforcement community. However, after negotiating throughout the legislative session, all parties involved and agreed on the principles of the final draft of the bill.

According to Watson (2006), the major issue debated by all parties related to the Tiers 1 and 2 requirements. The civil rights advocates including Senator West had originally proposed that all law enforcement agencies in Texas collect data on all contacts with citizens, including those related to pedestrians (Tier 2). This was perceived by the law enforcement community as a "monumental task" and one that they were not prepared to undertake. After much negotiation between all parties involved, it was agreed that all law enforcement agencies would be required to collect Tier 1 data (which includes only traffic-related contacts) but only those agencies that did not own video/audio equipment in patrol vehicles would be required to collect Tier 2 data (requirements to be explained in detail later on in this chapter). However, some agencies successfully argued that this exemption to the collection of Tier 2 data was unfair as there were numerous agencies in Texas that did not have the funds to purchase video/audio equipment. After much debate, it was decided that the Tier 2 exemption would also apply to agencies that had applied for state funding to be equipped with video/audio equipment, regardless of whether they had received the equipment; this decision seemed to satisfy law enforcement agencies. It is clear that none of the parties involved in these negotiations felt as if they had won a complete victory. However, most of the civil rights advocates felt that this constituted the first step in the "right" direction.

On March 5, 2001, Senator Royce West filed a bill before the Texas senate to "ban racial profiling among the law enforcement community in Texas." As stated previously, the language in the bill constituted a compromise among the different parties that had been involved in this particular effort. According to Senator West, "This is not the type of issue that will ever have 100 percent agreement on every point. But I appreciate the collaborative efforts of all those who have worked in good faith to reach this point" (West, 2001). It is widely believed that due to the compromise achieved before the bill was filed, the Texas senate did not express much opposition against the bill. In fact, the Senate Criminal Justice Committee, after hearing approximately two hours of testimony, voted 6–0 in favor of the bill. Once approved by the Criminal Justice Committee, the bill was introduced to the Texas senate, who soon thereafter approved it in its original form. It was then sent to the Texas House of Representatives, who passed it without much hesitation. However, the bill was slowed down by one of the congressional committee chairs who simply kept on rescheduling the final reading of the bill (ARC, 2001).

According to ARC (2001), the bill was scheduled for a final reading only after representatives from ACLU, LULAC, and NAACP held an impromptu sit-in outside the committee chair's office and refused to leave unless the bill was scheduled for a reading. The draft of the bill was finally approved by the Texas senate on April 4, 2001, on a 28–2 vote and it was subsequently signed into law by Texas Republican governor Rick Perry. According to the author of the bill, Senator Royce West, the bill constituted a " . . . giant step forward." He added that "both young and old African Americans and Hispanics come to me, and say, 'Senator, thank you for passing that bill.' Even though we must continue to lecture our sons and daughters about the hazards of driving while Black or Brown, it raises the hope that our rights and liberties will be protected and enforced under the laws of Texas" (West, 2001).

Despite the alleged consensus that existed regarding the language and the requirements introduced by the bill, the law enforcement community in Texas, for the most part, did not feel that the bill was necessary. Even though the bill became law in 2001 and was to take effect January 1, 2002, the interpretations made by each law enforcement agency in Texas regarding the requirements were different. Some argued that the bill did not have an enforcement mechanism and, thus, it was only meant to provide a sense of "good practices" among the Texas law enforcement community. Perhaps this was one of the most radical interpretations. Others, however, who seemed to be conscious of the fact the bill had now become law and was to be observed misinterpreted the Tier 2 exemption by arguing that if they had video and audio equipment in their patrol vehicles, they were exempt from collecting or reporting any traffic-stop data. Sadly, as the bill was passed with much haste, it did not have a chance to mature into the hearts and minds of the Texas law enforcement community. Thus, a great deal of confusion emerged throughout the state.

Despite the state of confusion on the newly established law, the Texas law enforcement community benefited from the expertise offered by the Law Enforcement Management Institute of Texas (LEMIT), based at the Sam Houston State University. All pertinent parties met under the leadership of its executive director, Dr. Rita Watkins. It seemed appropriate that an academic institute would serve as a neutral ground for all parties to work through the language of the final bill, which had to be translated into deliverables to the law enforcement community.

I became involved in this process as Dr. Watkins invited me to train, on behalf of the state of Texas, approximately 1,200 chiefs of police in the state over the course of two years. My primary mission was to train the law enforcement executives on matters relevant to racial profiling generally and on the Texas Law on Racial Profiling specifically. It was clear to me, early on, that the law enforcement community was very anxious about the requirements of the law and the legal implications this would bring to them. The notion that the law enforcement community, in general, is not flexible to change became clear when the law was introduced. Although reactions varied across the board, the general sense was of confusion and disbelief. The more seasoned chiefs of police expressed their disappointment about the new requirement, citing examples of how officers in other states had been "framed" by civil rights groups. They often mentioned to me that they were happy to know they were at the end of their career so this new requirement would only have a limited impact in their professional lives. Others who were not so seasoned expressed a willingness to abide by the law, understanding that this was a matter of career survivability, and some also felt that this was part of the notion of doing the right thing. Although they also seemed to hold some concerns similar to their seasoned counterparts', it was clear that they understood that the requirements of the racial profiling law were part of a new paradigm in policing. Most chiefs recognized that there was no other choice than understand and adhere to the law and its requirements and that not complying with the new law would result in the termination of their careers as police executives.

I also realized that despite years of experience, some in the law enforcement community seemed to have a naive understanding of the implications of data collection and analysis. While the police departments of five of the six major cities in Texas (Fort Worth, El Paso, Houston, San Antonio, and Austin) opted to collect Tier 2 data despite the exemption rule, a small number of agencies were of the opinion that there was no need to analyze data or collect information beyond the requirements specified by the law. Some police executives expressed their lack of interest in complying with the law, citing insufficient funds to conduct training sessions for their personnel or have outside consulting firms perform data analyses. The bottom line for these agencies was that the law did not contain any penalties for noncompliance and therefore they knew that no harm would come to their cities/agencies.

I want to make it clear that this group was small and constituted a minority of all law enforcement agencies in Texas, as most chiefs of police I met showed a strong desire to understand and adhere to the law. I often heard their request for further clarification as they provided examples of everyday occurrences facing a typical patrol officer. For the most part, these everyday occurrences were not referred to in the law; thus, it would be left up to the individual agency to interpret these specific instances and how they relate to the newly established requirements. Overall, the tone was positive and cautiously optimistic among most police agencies, as they held on to the hope that some of the "gray areas" of the law would be clarified at a later point.

Although I was not directly involved with patrol officers, it became obvious that their reaction was strong and, for the most part, negative toward the law. Some officers claimed that this law was passed by "liberals" in an attempt to destroy the law enforcement community. Others felt that they had "more important things to do" than to track data and make certain it was accurate. One officer told me that if he had wanted to become a statistician he would not have chosen law enforcement as a profession. It was interesting that some officers felt that the requirements established by the law were in some form manufactured by their chief of police. I often heard "the chief wants to micromanage all of us as he looks good before the city manager by asking us to collect every detail possible during the course of a traffic stop." I became convinced that some officers believed this of their chief due to lack of effective communication between command staff and patrol officers. In these cases, it was warranted that officers should become educated and informed on the history and nature of the law. This lack of communication resulted, in some cases, in an apparent decline in the number of traffic citations issued, which affected the overall revenues of cities whose budget is largely determined by the funds secured from traffic fines.

THE REQUIREMENTS OF THE TEXAS RACIAL PROFILING LAW

The Texas Racial Profiling Law included the same definition of racial profiling previously introduced by the federal government. The Texas Racial Profiling Law regarded racial profiling as "a law enforcement action based on an individual's race, ethnicity or national origin rather than on the individual's behavior or on information identifying the individual as having engaged in criminal activity" (Senate Bill 1074, 2001). Further, it established the following:

1. The prohibition of racial profiling among law enforcement agencies in Texas.
2. The adoption of a racial profiling policy by which police agencies were required to ban such practice among police officers.
3. Drafting and enforcing a complaint process relevant to racial profiling.
4. Launching an educational campaign aimed at informing the public of their right to complain on racial profiling abuses.
5. The submission of an annual traffic-contact report, by March 1 of each year, to the local governing body.
6. The collection of Tier 1 data by all agencies. This included the race/ethnicity of the contacts, searches (probable cause or consent), and arrests of all individuals who had an exchange with a police officer as a result of a traffic stop.
7. The collection of Tier 2 data by all agencies that did not own video/audio equipment in their vehicles. However, if the agency applied for funding from the state to purchase video/audio equipment, it was exempt from Tier 2 data requirements even if the monetary award was not issued by the State of Texas. Tier 2 requirements included, but were not exclusive of, all the requirements of Tier 1 in addition to data related to gender, location, nature of contraband, and other pertinent items.
8. All police personnel were required to receive a minimum of 8 hours of state-certified training on racial profiling. This was to be administered as an in-service course.
9. The requirement to report the number, nature, and final disposition of all written racial profiling complaints filed during the course of a calendar year. The law was specific in that it did not seek to obtain private records relevant to name of the alleged victim or of the officers alleged to have engaged in profiling.
10. The retention of video/audio tapes for a minimum of 90 days, during which time these were to be reviewed randomly.

Of all of these requirements, most law enforcement officers focused on the collection and reporting of traffic-contact data. They seem to have more questions about this requirement than any other. Perhaps this was due to the fact that they felt the data would either vindicate them or perhaps allow some to conclude that they were engaging in racial profiling. Regardless, there was a great deal of confusion regarding how to collect the data and what exactly was meant by ethnicity/race of a driver. Many officers asked then, and continue to ask today, how they are supposed to predict the exact race/ethnicity of the driver absent simply asking the person directly for this information. It should be noted that officers were discouraged, early on, from asking drivers for this information so that they would not become offended.

Perhaps one of the main challenges about the Texas Racial Profiling Law has to do with the fact that it did not contain specific instructions on most items required from the law enforcement community. For instance, with regard to the launching of an "educational campaign," most law enforcement agencies had questions regarding how they could satisfy this specific item. That is, what does it mean to "launch" an "educational campaign"? Some felt that this requirement implied that they advertise, in their local newspaper, the manner in which people could file a complaint based on racial profiling. Others, however, felt that this was way too aggressive and opted to make available in the lobby area of their police departments a handout that contained information on filing a complaint. In other instances, chiefs of police opted to post their racial profiling complaint policy on their departmental websites. This posed a problem, in some instances, as some of the constituents in these specific areas of Texas did not have access to the Internet. Further, the information posted on the website was hard to find even by those who claimed to be familiar with the online environment.

Another example of the ambiguity of the requirements relates to the issue of "contacts." The law required the collection of contacts that originate from a traffic stop. Though its interpretation may seem simple to some, it became a very difficult issue for law enforcement to understand. Specifically, some police agencies that did not understand the meaning of a contact counted each citation issued. This inflated their data as some individuals who came in contact with the police only once may have received multiple citations during the same incident. Others regarded a contact as any exchange that an officer would have with a citizen despite the fact this person may or may not be involved in a traffic-related event. The law specifically referenced a contact as one which resulted from a traffic-related stop and where an individual received a citation or was arrested. Again, a debate emerged as to the meaning of a "citation." Some argued that a citation included a warning, which is exclusively a component of the Tier 2 requirement, while others agreed that a citation excludes warnings as part of the Tier 1 requirement. The latter was the correct interpretation but clearly this issue seems to have confused most law enforcement agencies.

Law enforcement agencies in Texas are also required to submit the total number of contacts in a given year while controlling for race and ethnicity. The law made it clear that each agency had to report the total number and percentage of individuals of Caucasian, African American, Hispanic, Asian, and Native American descent who came in contact with the police. Further, the total number and type of searches, in addition to the number of arrests made, had to be reported by race/ethnicity. The problem lies in the fact that police officers, when making a contact with a citizen, do not always correctly predict the race and/or ethnicity of the individual. Thus, there are oftentimes when the officer relies on instinct when recording the contact as being of a particular race/ethnicity. For instance, an officer may regard a citizen as Hispanic even if the individual may be a female whose first name is "Cindy" and appears to be Caucasian, but has a Spanish surname (e.g., Gonzales, Ramirez, Gutierrez). In other cases, officers relied on the Department of Public Safety computer system, which does not include Hispanics and combines this group with Caucasians. Thus, when this fact was presented by the press, citizens began to file complaints arguing that some police departments were "hiding" behind the numbers by excluding Hispanics—a major violation of the requirements of the Texas Racial Profiling Law.

With regard to searches, the law requires that all probable cause (PC) and consent searches that originate from a traffic contact be recorded. The primary reason why this requirement may have caused confusion lies in the fact that police officers perform additional types of searches. For instance, if an individual is stopped by an officer and after verifying the information on the driver's license the officer finds out that the person is wanted for a couple of outstanding warrants, the individual may end up being arrested and the vehicle searched under the "inventory search" premise. That is, the vehicle is inventoried to make sure that all property in it will be counted so that when the vehicle is returned to its owner, it contains the same property. However, if the officer finds contraband in the course of the inventory search, it may be used against the suspect in a court of law. The issue that led to confusing figures relevant to the PC and consent search requirement is that some police departments added to the search total inventory searches as well. Given this, some police departments ended up reporting information that was not accurate and probably exaggerated their total number of searches. Others included, in the total searches reported, instances when the officer did not have any discretion in arresting the suspect and performing a search. Unfortunately, the law did not address these special conditions or circumstances that are often present in the law enforcement environment.

As mentioned earlier, the Texas Racial Profiling Law also required the collection and reporting of arrests that came about in the course of a traffic-related contact. Again, there was a great deal of confusion when considering which arrests should be reported. Although officers were clear that arrests that took place once they had made a contact with the suspect for a traffic-related circumstance were to be reported, many wondered if they had to report instances when the suspect had a warrant for his/her arrest and the officer did not exhibit any discretion when making the arrest. Also, some officers wondered if they should count arrests that originate from a traffic stop but end up taking place due to contraband being found or some other criminal act discovered once the stop had been made.

The Texas Racial Profiling Law required that police agencies submit an annual report to their local governing body by March 1 of each year. Some police chiefs interpreted this requirement as one where they had to make a presentation before their city council regarding racial profiling. These presentations were, for the most part, controversial and filled with questions about what the police department was doing right or wrong. Some city council members, for the sake of reminding their constituents that they were "fighting a good cause," asked to the chiefs making the presentation questions that were almost impossible to respond or that were inaccurate in nature. Police chiefs who had seen this as a career-making opportunity were quickly awakened by the fact that their presentations were typically interrupted by politically loaded city council members who were out to make a name for themselves. Perhaps the more seasoned police chiefs opted to submit the report in the "working session" of city councils, with a note asking them to submit questions to the chief directly in case they had any after reading the report. These questions were seldom submitted and the political debate regarding racial profiling was typically contained.

With regard to the review of the video/audio equipment requirement, this did not seem to be the cause of much discussion until it was learned that some agencies were not reviewing the tapes randomly but were, in fact, reviewing tapes sporadically or exclusively when a complaint was filed. However, this was short-lived as agencies began to recognize the value in digital technology and began acquiring video/audio equipment so that recordings could be stored for more than the minimum requirement of 90 days. Some agencies also learned to record the times in which they reviewed the videos in order to establish record and show that this requirement was also met.

As you can imagine, the politics affecting the issue of racial profiling in Texas were present since the idea was first discussed among politicians and civil rights leaders and before the bill was drafted. It is hard to imagine that such a controversial topic would not have political ramifications. The topic of racial profiling touches a nerve among minorities in that it serves as a constant reminder of the civil rights struggle. Further, it also serves as a topic of choice for reporters who constantly look for the "hot news" to cover. It is hard to imagine a reporter who would not like to have his/her name associated with the headline "Police Department Engages in Racial Profiling of Motorists" or perhaps "Blacks and Hispanics Are More Likely to Be Stopped and Issued a Citation in Our City." In addition, police agencies, who are often under fire for their racial profiling/traffic-contact figures, also have a defensive attitude the issue of racial profiling. This, added to the political dimensions of the topic, makes it into a rather difficult issue for police agencies to counter. I once heard a chief of police tell me that "before the fight started, police agencies across the nation had already lost." This meant that they would not be afforded an opportunity to explain their figures in a rather difficult environment, where the public, aided by civil rights leaders, would "demand" explanations given the racial profiling figures reported.

It was clear to me, since the beginning of the racial profiling debate in Texas, that the topic would grow in unprecedented political dimensions. I, however, ignored, to some extent, the political dimensions of the topic until I was invited to make a presentation on racial profiling by a group called the Texas Reform Coalition. This group represented agencies such as the ACLU, the LULAC, and the NAACP. I attended the one-day conference which was held in Austin, Texas, in Spring, 2003. The idea was to hold a conference where all sides could be heard on the topic; since I had been training chiefs of police on racial profiling, they felt it would be appropriate to invite me to present my particular perspective.

After listening to other researchers who discussed the definition of racial profiling and the challenges that data collection posed, it became clear to me that this topic had a different meaning/relevance to each party represented at the conference. To some, in the civil rights arena, this meant the "new civil rights cause" which was to be won at all costs regardless of whether or not the data and its interpretation made much sense from a statistical perspective. To law enforcement officers, this was yet another way for liberals to take their power and authority away. Thus, they had to fight this battle at all costs since it represented a direct attack on their role in society. Before characterizing the perspective of researchers, I would argue that there were two types of researchers who were present at the conference. One group was made up of individuals who serve as consultants and clearly regard this issue as one that has the potential of generating substantial income. The other type of researcher relates to the academic who explores this topic further and attempts to come up with "new" perspectives or angles on the topic as a means of making a contribution to the relevant body of knowledge (by seeing it implemented first hand in the field). Of these two, most of the audience present was receptive to the traditional academic who did not see this as a source of monetary gain.

It became clear to me, at the conference, that none of the parties involved were really interested in the concepts that were statistically sound. Most disregarded this discussion as being irrelevant to their specific perspective. When I attempted to explain that the Fair Roads Standard, a baseline proposed by the civil rights groups, was simply not the best measure to use as it relied on census information on heads of households that had access to vehicles and not people that drove, some claimed that I was attempting to "confuse" things. Others, however, seemed to understand the argument and asked the question that I was not able to answer—"What other options do you suggest?" Clearly, there are not many baseline options available and as discussed in the previous chapter, most of these pose statistical limitations. It was obvious that, to some, I was not too friendly to the agenda they had worked so hard to promote. Since the agenda for the conference was largely created by the civil rights groups, during lunch, a few individuals made a presentation claiming that they had been the subject of racial profiling. It was clear from their presentation that they had been victims of this horrible act and I agreed with the notion that it was important to disseminate this information to the public, particularly chiefs of police, some of whom were also present. However, I was not in agreement with some who, after listening to the anecdotes describing racial profiling acts on behalf of law enforcement officers, felt the need to make the point that this was also happening across the board in Texas. I felt that these comments were not substantiated by any fact and had the tendency of polarizing the chiefs of police from other members of the community, resulting in greater possibilities for the "racial divide" to continue.

After the conference ended, we were not any closer to an agreement or a general understanding of each other's perspectives. However, I became fully aware, after the conference, of the differences of opinion that existed among different groups in Texas. I remember thinking on the three-hour drive back to Dallas that this topic was clearly an example of a social problem being transferred to the law enforcement community. Further, it was a social problem that academics tried to explain and provide some direction but whose efforts were subject to the scrutiny of both sides, who often interpreted the academic findings provided in the literature to serve their particular perspectives. It became clear that we would not come up with an answer or a consensus anytime soon. Therefore, the role of academics became one of assisting law enforcement agencies and the civil rights groups in defining the terms or guidelines that would allow us to determine which agency was in compliance with the law. However, once the compliance issue had been resolved, it would be left up to each municipality to interpret their findings according to their own viewpoint, using their own statistical tools. These viewpoints were often challenged by the findings produced by researchers working for civil rights groups; they used their own statistical formulas to support the point that most agencies (or at least a large number) were engaging in racial profiling across the state of Texas.

After the first year of collecting and reporting their racial profiling data before city councils, boards, and commissioners, the Texas law enforcement community was surprised when they received open records requests to submit their racial profiling data to the Texas Reform Coalition. This organization, in an attempt to collect information and report it in a comprehensive manner, filed open record requests with almost every law enforcement agency in Texas. Although not every agency complied with this request, the Texas Reform Coalition was able to draft a report with the assistance of Dr. Dwight Steward, an accomplished academic and former professor of Economics at the University of Texas at Austin. The report contained totals and percentages while controlling for race and ethnicity as reported by agencies regarding traffic stops made by officers. This allowed the reader to find out, for instance, how many African Americans had been stopped in Dallas, while comparing this figure to the total number of Caucasians stopped in the same city. Further, the report allowed readers to determine the number of individuals searched and those arrested as a result of a traffic stop.

From a researcher's perspective, the report was very interesting and highlighted important points for discussion. However, most law enforcement officials regarded the report as not representative of the efforts made by their officers. Further, they questioned publicly and privately the figures and statistical measures employed in the analysis of data. The report was widely covered by news organizations across the United States. The major news sources, both in print and on television, covered the release of the report, while affirming that racial profiling was a problem in Texas. This clearly infuriated police chiefs, whose concern was that their personal reputation and that of their cities and officers was being challenged. The end result was a direct response to the report by attacking the methodology used and presenting news releases from large police agencies in the state, which affirmed that racial profiling was not a major concern and that they had their own figures to report that would counter the ones produced by the civil rights groups.

I found myself in the middle of the controversy as police chiefs called on me to "make sense of the numbers." My advice to them was to collect more data in order to explain the full picture of the traffic-stop data patterns. I often argued that if one says "25 percent of contacts are made with Blacks" in a given city, it fails to recognize what this means given the fact that some of the individuals that came in contact may be from other cities and therefore not represented in the census data—a typical source of comparison. Further, it may be the case that police officers are stopping individuals who may have broken the law irrespective of race and ethnicity. These explanations do not remove the argument that racial profiling may also take place; however, they point out the fact that a mere figure does not conclusively present evidence one way or the other that racial profiling has occurred.

In subsequent years, the civil rights groups continued to file open record requests to police agencies in Texas and additional reports were created. However, the most recent reports seem to have focused on searches conducted as a result of a traffic stop. Specifically, the findings presented in these reports suggest that searches of minorities are being conducted disproportionately when compared to Caucasian searches. In keeping with the conflicting views on this topic, many law enforcement agencies have regarded these recent findings as biased and incomplete. Advocates of law enforcement agencies argue that the findings relevant to searches don't tell the whole story as they simply ignore the fact that there is no way to statistically determine the percentage of individuals who deserved to be searched. Thus, there is no comparative baseline for search figures.

The Texas legislature meets every other year. During the last legislative session, Senator Royce West, originally responsible for introducing Senate Bill 1074, attempted to introduce new legislation aimed at "putting teeth" behind the current law. Specifically, the bill introduced proposed the creation of a central repository, which was to be housed by an academic institution in North Texas whose satellite campus was under the senator's jurisdiction. Further, the bill did away with the Tier 2 exemption, thus mandating that all law enforcement agencies report Tiers 1 and 2 information regardless of the fact that they may have video/audio equipment or may have applied for funds to purchase this equipment. In addition, it was proposed that all law enforcement agencies should provide identifiable information on officers and a report of the race/ethnicity of the individuals they had come in contact with during the course of traffic/pedestrian stops during a given year. This clearly touched a nerve among law enforcement groups in the state of Texas, resulting in a major lobbying campaign aimed at derailing the proposed bill. Further, the bill proposed to apply penalties on those agencies that failed to report racial profiling data as required by law.

Although the bill was passed during the third reading at the Texas senate, it had a different set of requirements once passed. That is, it did away with language relevant to the repository at an academic institution and with the requirements relevant to specific individual officer information regarding their stops. Although it still required a repository, it proposed the Department of Public Safety as the logical place where all yearly data should be stored. Further, it contained language that was much more lenient and less restrictive. The bill, once passed in the senate, arrived in the Urban Affairs Committee in the Texas House of Representatives. The legislative session ended before the Committee conducted the expected hearing on the bill. Thus, it never became law.

At the time of writing there are suspicions that the upcoming legislative session in Texas will once again revisit the racial profiling law and consider introducing a bill which aims at providing further restrictions on the data being collected and the manner in which it is being reported. It is unclear if the bill will be introduced or if legislators will support it. Nevertheless, it is clear that the racial profiling debate is far from ending in Texas. As such, the struggle for disclosure and fair presentation of traffic-stop data continues.

This chapter deals with the Texas experience in an attempt to illustrate the different issues that arise in states as they consider the implementation of racial profiling laws and when the laws are executed. Some have argued that Texas is regarded by civil rights groups as a turf where the racial profiling debate, at a national level, is to begin. The reasons are obvious: It is one of the largest and most conservative states with a historical reputation (whether or not it is deserving) on lack of tolerance toward minorities. It is also the state where the now famous Jasper incident, involving the violent death of an African American man, took place not too long ago. These and other similar incidents have placed Texas in the midst of the racial divide generally and racial profiling specifically. It has been my experience to hear when conversing with officers, civil rights activists, and researchers from others states that the Texas experience is also their own.

References

Applied Research Center (ARC) (2001). *Preventing Racial Profiling by Police*. SB 1074, State of Texas, 2001.

King, Joyce (2002). *Hate Crime: The Story of Dragging in Jasper*. Texas: Pantheon.

Nate, Blakeslee (2005). *Tulia: Race, Cocaine, and Corruption in a Small Texas Town*. Public Affairs.

Senate Bill 1074 (2001). 77th Texas Legislature. 2001.

Watson, Rick (2006). Public Information Officer. Dallas Police Department. Phone Interview. September 1, 2006.

West, Royce (2001). Texas State Senator. District 23. Press Release. May 21, 2001.

CHAPTER 7

Racial Profiling in the Era of Homeland Security

The terrorist attacks of September 11, 2001 (9/11), made a profound impact on the United States and its citizens. Although the portion of the landscape that has been forever changed by the attacks of 9/11 is small, it is clear that a significant impact took place in the psyche of the American public. Soon after these terrorist attacks, some Americans expressed fear of flying as they replayed in their mind images of airplanes colliding against buildings in New York City and the Pentagon. The American public woke up to a different world stage. The voices of America's political figures came together in a unified manner to proclaim that the time to act was now, and we were the generation to respond to the greatest threat the United States has ever faced—terrorism.

Although the political and military response involved the invasion of Afghanistan, and later Iraq, most people in the United States returned to their daily routine with a sense of pain and also with a desire to "react" to the attacks of 9/11. In some areas of the country, Americans opted to expand their homes as they decided to forego their out of town trips and exchange these for a more comfortable setting at home. Others bought weapons as they sought feelings of security and safety. It was clear, from all accounts, that Americans opted to stay home, expand their immediate area of residency, and purchase items that made them feel safer. It has been estimated that a baby-boom population, born 9 months after 9/11, is yet another phenomenon which emerged since 9/11.

With regard to the social response toward individuals of ethnic descent, soon after 9/11, passengers at airports began to report to authorities that they should detain individuals who, in their view, resembled those who had been featured on television as having performed the terrorist attacks against the United States. In some cases, passengers asked authorities to de-board fellow passengers who were visibly Muslim or had a Middle Eastern affiliation.

One of the most visible cases where racial profiling took place involved California congressman Darrell Issa, the grandson of Lebanese immigrants. Congressman Issa claims to have been the subject of racial profiling at Dulles airport in Washington DC, as an Air France counter agent refused to let him get on the flight destined to the Middle East (Orange County Register, 2001). It appears that when Congressman Issa, who was accompanied by Representative Robert Wexler of Florida, arrived at Dulles, the airline agent entered Issa's name on the computer and told him to wait. Soon after, the agent arrived back and said, "You are flying tomorrow." Issa replied, "you have got to be kidding" as the agent started to blame the Federal Aviation Administration and its rules. However, when questioned, the agent blamed the French authorities and did not offer any additional explanation as to why Issa would not be allowed to fly on that day. At the end of the ordeal, the airliner offered no explanation as to why they did not allow the congressman to board the plane except that Mr. Issa arrived within 50 minutes before departure and this was considered to be too late. However, records show that Mr. Issa arrived earlier and that according to the policy of the airliner, passengers should arrive at least 45 minutes before departure (Orange County Register, 2001). Regardless, this case was one of the first to receive national attention as an instance where racial profiling was in effect only days after the attacks of September 11, 2001.

RACIAL PROFILING TRENDS

Similar incidents were taking place all over the United States. In Michigan, a group of boy scouts were also victims of racial profiling. On September 15, 2001, on Mackinac Island a group of Arab American teenagers and their Boy Scout leader were subject to the scrutiny of local residents, who called the Mackinac city police to report a group of "suspicious-looking people." According to the call received by the police, local residents reported a group of suspicious people who were speaking in a foreign language and were using walkie-talkies while taking pictures of the Mackinac Bridge (Detroit Free Press, 2001). That day, the scout leader was wearing a camouflage jacket, which also added to the suspicion.

According to reports, the local authorities questioned the group of Boy Scouts and despite the fact they were ready to release them after a short while, the FBI, who were alerted of the event, wanted the boys to be held in custody until they arrived and had a chance to speak to them. The boys were noticeably scared and they had been apparently speaking to each other on walkie-talkies so that no one would get lost during their camping trip. After the FBI arrived, the boys were set free but not without much frustration on their part. In the words of the Boy Scout leader, who was also held for suspicious activity—"the people who did the World Trade Center, they're intruders to Islam . . . no one ethnic or religious group should be singled out because of this" (Detroit Free Press, 2001).

Another case involved the denial of an Arab American secret service agent, who was part of the presidential detail, to board an American Airlines plane. On December 28, 2001, in advancement of President Bush's Christmas trip to his Crawford ranch, an armed

Arab American secret service agent was denied to board an American Airlines plane from the Baltimore-Washington airport to the Dallas-Fort Worth airport. The reasons for denying his entrance to the plane were never made clear other than that the pilot of that particular flight did not feel comfortable allowing this individual to board the plane. The official pronouncement was that the pilot, in accordance with airline safety rules, reviewed the documentation produced by the agent and felt that it would be in everyone's best interests that the agent did not board the plane. However, the agent felt that it was due to his race/ethnicity that he was forbidden to board the plane (Houston Chronicle, 2001). Clearly, this was yet one more incident where race/ethnicity played a role in the conclusion, by an individual or an organization, that safety was compromised given a person's racial makeup.

It is clear that racial profiling was and still is a factor to consider given that the 9/11 terrorists were Arabs. Clearly, people in a crisis or emergency state tend to fear that which is unknown to them. Thus, the reaction to the 9/11 events was to become suspicious of anyone who would resemble any or all of those 19 men who were responsible for the deaths of thousands of Americans. However, it is not logical to experience racial/ethnic fear due to this: Only 19 men committed this horrible act, while approximately 3 million Arab Americans live in the United States, most of whom will never be involved in a terrorist act. Despite the lack of logic here, it is clear that soon after the attacks of 9/11, some Americans engaged in racial profiling. As mentioned earlier, newspaper reports relating stories of passengers refusing to board airplanes that were also occupied by Arab American passengers were abundant (*Newsweek*, 2001). In retrospect, this is clearly the wrong approach to take on the issue of terrorism; however, many people claim that this was only a natural reaction by a country that was still in disbelief of a criminal act of unprecedented magnitude.

As you may recall from previous chapters, the campaign to end racial profiling did not start after September 11, 2001. In fact, the federal initiative to end racial profiling was initiated by President Clinton in 1999. However, many individuals in the law enforcement profession and some academic circles predicted, inaccurately, that racial profiling would end after 9/11, since most Americans would come to agree that it did not matter if race was combined in a formula to prohibit certain people from flying, as long as the United States remained safe. I remember, in particular, a chief of police saying that no one cared anymore (after 9/11) about the issue of racial profiling, since we were all trying to come together as a nation in order to fight a common enemy.

The issue, however, was that no one knew then (and perhaps still don't know today) who exactly is our enemy. Most Americans heard of al-Qaeda and Osama bin Laden but this information is rather limited and superficial. Thus, the problem is that some people who have not been exposed to other cultures or who perhaps don't enjoy a strong intellectual background on matters related to terrorism feel that anyone who "looks Muslim or Arab" must be a terrorist. This tendency has transcended to public policy, by which security experts in certain airports are allowed to profile passengers on the basis of a series of factors, some of which include race and ethnicity. Thus, one could argue that racial profiling is alive and well in the era of homeland security. Further, one could agree with the notion that if racial profiling was a concern before 9/11, it should now be a greater source of attention in the era of homeland security, when the freedom and rights of citizens appear to be on a fragile platform.

It is said that we learn more through visual images than through any other method of learning. If this is in fact true, it should not be surprising to learn of the impact of the terrorist attacks of 9/11 as most of the images related to these attacks were shown live on television to a wide audience. Given the tragic nature of these images, people in the United States began to experience a public panic which was based on fear. The fear of the unknown and the feeling of vulnerability led the American people to support initiatives proposed by the U.S. government to fight terrorism. If these initiatives had been proposed at any other time in the history of this nation, they would have never been discussed, much less passed in a legislative body. However, given the traumatic state of the United States and its people, America was ready to respond in an "emotional" manner to the threat of terrorism. This response led to certain initiatives, including, but not exclusive of, modified airport security, the Patriot Act, and the enforcement of profiles by U.S. Customs officials.

AIRPORT SECURITY AND RACIAL PROFILING

The first item discussed, as a possible reform, after the 9/11 terrorist attacks involved airport security. Considering that airports served as the location where the terrorist attacks of 9/11 were initiated, it is not surprising that security efforts have focused on airports across the United States. As you can imagine, given the strict security measures, airports have also experienced a large number of issues relevant to profiling. Specifically, claims have been made that at airports security personnel engage in racial profiling and use the shield of homeland security to justify their actions.

In fact, from July 2003 to August 2004, the Amnesty International's Domestic Human Rights Program studied racial profiling by law enforcement agencies throughout the United States generally and focused, among other areas, on airport security specifically. The process started in fall 2003, in consultation with a wide range of community organizations and a series of public hearings across the United States. During these hearings, human rights advocates, victims, law enforcement officials, and experts testified about their own experiences regarding racial profiling.

The hearings were followed by supporting research material which focused on:

1. State laws concerning racial profiling.
2. The U.S. Supreme Court's interpretation of relevant protections provided by the U.S. Constitution.
3. Relevant federal policies.
4. International treaties, covenants, and laws.
5. National public opinion polls.
6. Review of the U.S. census data.

7. A comprehensive review of the literature relevant to racial profiling (Amnesty International, 2006).

The major findings of the study were as follows:

1. A staggering number of people in the United States are subjected to racial profiling. Specifically, almost 32 million Americans (the equivalent of the population of Canada) reported to have been victimized by racial profiling.
2. Approximately 87 million Americans are at a high risk of being subjected to future racial profiling acts during their lifetime.
3. Racial profiling directly affects individuals of minority descent, including Native Americans, Asians, Hispanics, African Americans, Arabs, Persians, and Muslims, and under specific circumstances, Caucasians.
4. Racial profiling occurs to both women and men, affecting all age groups, and it is used against people from all socioeconomic backgrounds. In addition, it occurs in rural, suburban, and urban areas (Amnesty International, 2006).

Although this study did not focus on any particular type of racial profiling, it included information related to racial profiling at airports. According to the Amnesty International Report (2006), racial profiling at airports has widely increased since the terrorist attacks of September 11, 2001. This is particularly true of Muslims or individuals of Middle Eastern descent. The report cites anecdotes about racial profiling. Some of these are as follows:

In Tulsa, Dr. Sandra Rana, a member of the Tulsa Police Community Race Relations Committee, told the Amnesty International group that her family was targeted at an airport. Specifically, Dr. Rana claims that airport security officials pulled her eight-year-old son from the line and took apart the Boy Scout pinewood derby car he had built. Her son, Omar, is, according to Dr. Rana, often targeted at airports. Dr. Rana narrates the incident as follows:

> Imagine how I felt when my eight year old son was pulled from the line because of his name and I could not go with him. Imagine how he felt when they started to take apart his Boy Scout pinewood derby car in the Boy Scout box. . . . It is now routine for my son, for Omar Rana, to get extra security checks at airports. He knows it's going to happen, and he expects it. . . . But how do I tell my . . . son that it's okay? He is now ten. He is learning about civil liberties and civil rights. What meaning do they have for him . . .? Upon advice from law enforcement officials, Dr. Rana has stooped wearing her hijab to the airport (hijab is the traditional Muslim head covering for women). It's not just the scarf. I tell my kids, don't speak Urdu. It's the Pakistani language. Don't speak it when you are on the plane. Don't take the Quran. We've have [been] advised by officials, do not carry any book that's in Arabic. . . . Don't do anything that will cause attention to yourself. (Amnesty International, 2006.)

The story of Dr. Rana is not unique or isolated. In fact, newspapers across the United States continue to report incidents related to racial profiling. For instance, on October 8, 2001, Muhammed Ali, a Pakistani-born engineer with Lucent Technologies, boarded an airline at Boston's Logan Airport on his way home to Washington DC. However, minutes before take off, airline security personnel called him from the airplane. As soon as he stepped off the airplane, FBI agents proceeded to interview him while checking his background. He was finally declared safe to fly once the interview was conducted. However, the pilot refused to allow Ali to board the airplane, while directing the flight attendants to block the entrance of the airplane as Ali attempted to board the plane. Ali ultimately returned home safely on another flight approximately 3 hours later (Dade, 2002).

The point to consider here is that there are approximately 40 million people in the United States who travel by air in a given year. Thus, it is virtually impossible to stop each one of them and make an individual assessment in order to determine risk. However, some disagree. According to Professor Turley of the George Washington University Law School, "We have to develop some type of profile. The fact is, profiling is a legitimate statistical device. And it's a device that we may have to use if we're going to have a meaningful security process at these airports" (Leiser, 2002). Although profiling may be considered a useful tool for law enforcement, it is flawed and far from perfect. Further, it should never use race as a predictor as it is bound to fail in its attempt to fight/prevent terror.

For instance, if we were to use race and ethnicity as a predictor when profiling individuals in order to prevent a terrorist attack against the United States, it would be rather easy for a terrorist group to identify this and simply rely on someone who may not fit the racial and ethnic profile being sought by the government. For instance, contacting someone who belongs to a racist organization in the United States and influencing this person to commit a terrorist attack.

Consider the fact that three of the most famous accused terrorists today do not fit a racial/ethnic profile that seeks to identify individuals of Middle Eastern descent. That is, John Walker Lindh is a White American; Zacarias Moussaoui is an African with a French passport; and Jose Padilla, a Hispanic American. They are all Muslims but they are from different racial/ethnic backgrounds, none of which originate in the Middle East.

According to Norman Y. Mineta, in his statement before the U.S. Commission on Civil Rights (2001),

> While safety and security are of the highest concern to [the Department of Transportation], we also understand the nature of the Nation our efforts are designated to protect: a society that respects civil and constitutional rights and cherishes the values of equal justice and equal opportunity. As one of the 120,000 Americans of Japanese ancestry interned by the United States government during World War II, I know firsthand the dangers with which we are presented in the current crisis. All of us will face heightened security in the aftermath of September 11, but the security and scrutiny must never become pretext for unlawful discrimination.

The notion that racial profiling is a necessity to secure the nation is simply not accurate. Further, it suggests that people of particular ethnic backgrounds are more likely to engage in terrorism than others. This, again, is not accurate. Despite this, racial profiling at airports has found support among individuals whose cultural ignorance is evident.

It is interesting to note the obvious contradictions that exist between federal and local law enforcement agencies throughout the United States. It is often the case that we read stories in our local newspapers describing a new profiling program in place at a local airport; however, despite the federal move to include race as a method of detection, local authorities seem to be disconnected from the federal mandates to profiling individuals. I spoke to a chief of police about this subject and he cited a conversation he had with a federal agent who encouraged him to direct his officers to "gather intelligence" in areas of town heavily populated by people of Middle Eastern descent. The chief mentioned that he simply ignored this directive as he felt that this would open the door for lawsuits to be filed, at which time the federal government would likely not assist the city in seeking relief.

USA PATRIOT ACT AND RACIAL PROFILING

In addition to airport security, racial profiling seems to have been a component of the USA PATRIOT Act. Soon after the terrorist attacks of 9/11, the U.S. government passed legislature with the aim of lessening the restrictions on law enforcement agencies as they identified and investigated suspects of terrorism. The rationale was that by cutting the "red tape," law enforcement agencies would have the "edge" necessary to fight terrorism. The new legislation, known by the acronym USA PATRIOT Act, was passed nearly unanimously in the U.S. Senate by 98–1 and 357–66 in the House. The Patriot Act is made up of multiple sections, some of which:

1. Allow investigators to use the tools already in place to investigate organized crime groups and drug trafficking when investigating members of terrorist organizations.
2. Allow law enforcement to use surveillance when investigating terrorists.
3. Enable law enforcement agents to follow sophisticated terrorists by relying on roving wiretaps.
4. Allow law enforcement officers to perform investigations without having to tip off terrorists.
5. Enable law enforcement personnel to obtain business records in terrorism cases involving security terrorism.
6. Facilitate information sharing and cooperation among governmental agencies in order to work cohesively toward a common goal.
7. Allow for law enforcement officers to use new technologies in the assessment of threats.
8. Allow officials to obtain a search warrant anywhere a terrorist-related activity took place.
9. Enable victims of computer hacking to request law enforcement assistance in monitoring those trespassing their computers.
10. Increase the penalties related to individuals convicted of committing terrorist crimes.
11. Prohibit the harboring of terrorists.
12. Increase maximum penalties for crimes likely to have been committed by terrorists.

13. Increase the maximum penalties for conspiracies.

14. Enable to punish terrorist attacks on mass transit systems.

15. Enable to punish bioterrorists.

16. Eliminate the status of limitation for certain terrorism crimes and lengthen them for other terrorist crimes (U.S. Department of Justice, 2002).

These are some of the components of the Patriot Act, and they highlight some of the major powers issued to law enforcement on behalf of the U.S. government in order to engage in the war on terror. Although I would never argue against the idea that giving tools to law enforcement is the right move toward effective crime control (in this case, the control of terrorism), it should be noted that these powers also tend to widen the discretion of law enforcement officials. The point here is that widening the discretion of law enforcement officers tends to allow some to engage in illegal and unethical practices such as racial profiling. For instance, if an officer is given more freedom and less scrutiny, that particular individual, if prone to racial tendencies, could engage more freely in racist behavior, including, but not exclusive of, racial profiling

It is not clear as to how the powers enacted by the act should be used. The selective identification and apprehension of individuals based on factors other than criminality, such as political affinity and religious or ethnic origin, is a possibility, as those that interpret the powers given by the Patriot Act can feel compelled to think that racial profiling is simply one more tool in the war on terror. Even if you don't believe that this could take place, it is clear to all of us that the enactment of such legislature creates the impression among some that we must protect the homeland at all cost—even if this means sacrificing the most vital constitutional rights.

It should be noted that the original Patriot Act contained provisions that allowed it to function only for a few years (sunset clause). The rationale for doing this was that at some point legislators could begin to question the wisdom of this act and therefore change their minds with regard to the provisions contained. However, before the sunset clause ended, the U.S. Congress passed legislation to ratify the Patriot Act and also to expand its scope of influence. It should not be surprising for us to learn, then, that the expansion of the act has resulted in the introduction of legal action against the government by interest groups whose arguments have focused on the notion that civil rights violations are occurring daily as a result of the newly introduced components of the act. (Read more about the USA PATRIOT Act by visiting the Department of Homeland Security's website at http://www.dhs.gov.)

U.S. CUSTOMS AND RACIAL PROFILING

Another area of focus, as we consider racial profiling during the era of homeland security, relates to alleged racial profiling practices by U.S. Customs agents. Although it is believed that these practices are, for the most part, no longer in place, it is important to examine these further. Specifically, we should focus on several cases that emerged from Chicago's O'Hare airport, as claims were made that U.S. Customs agents had made unjustifiable searches on individuals of African American descent.

While employed as a customs agent, whistle-blower Cathy Harris observed the following unwritten rules to target African American passengers:

a. Having an "Afrocentric name"
b. Live in low income areas
c. Live in high narcotic areas
d. Have a low paying job
e. If you are unemployed
f. Wearing bulky/baggy clothing
g. Wearing African attire
h. Wearing "Afrocentric" hairstyles
i. Wearing any type of headgear, whether it is a wig, hat, scarf, etc.
j. Wearing thick-soled shoes
k. Purchased ticket in cash
l. Purchased ticket one or two days prior to trip
m. Went on short trip
n. If you are a "frequent traveler"
o. If you are "traveling alone"
p. If you are carrying only one piece of luggage
q. Unusual or inconsistent itinerary
r. Traveling from a "source country"?
s. If you act nervous
t. If you have a foreign accent or a foreign "look," specially Caribbean or African descent
u. If you are too polite or argumentative
v. If you are wearing sunglasses
w. If you are acting ill (Galbraith, 2001)

Although it would be hard to imagine by most of us that a responsible governmental entity would rely on such nonscientific information, it is in fact the case that these items served as "guidelines" for stopping individuals deemed as "suspicious." This was particularly true of African Americans. One of the reasons as to why this is accepted by the public is that most people believe this may be part of an effective targeting process. That is, most people would agree that illegal immigration comes from Mexico and that most drug traffickers arrive from Colombia. Thus, it is not hard to imagine why there is support for the notion that individuals from "certain" countries with "particular" features should indeed be targeted by customs officials. It is also important to note that the list provided earlier is one that includes some features/items beyond those related to race and ethnicity. This makes it easier for customs officials to defend in court if accused of racial profiling. Finally, the liability incurred by those using the unwritten rules is almost never going to be subject to court challenges from the countries in which these passengers originated. This is due to the fact laws vary in each country and some nations probably believe that selective enforcement of the law, including racial profiling, may be acceptable.

According to Galbraith (2001), customs officials are taught to single out African Americans generally and black women specifically as the "culmination of a well thought out logic that is coded to disguise itself." That is, customs inspectors are directed to identify class incongruities—meaning, how passengers' outward appearance does not match or agree with their socioeconomic position (Galbraith, 2001). For instance, "Does the jewelry worn fit the social and economic status of the passenger?" The manual asks if the gold Rolex watch worn by an unemployed man matches his socioeconomic status? Clearly, the answer to this question is "no"; thus, according to instructions, this person should be stopped and asked questions. The problem with this logic is that many inspectors at O'Hare airport, as discovered by a lawsuit, have a blue-collar mentality that blacks in particular cannot afford to travel internationally, and that this particular destination is really reserved for Hollywood types (Galbraith, 2001).

In one instance, according to Galbraith (2001), Inspector Rocha at O'Hare wanted to know how Yvette Casey "could afford to take such a 'long vacation' despite the fact her trip to Jamaica only lasted a week." Also, when Arcaida Letkemann passed through customs at O'Hare in 1996, a customs inspector proceeded to ask her "how does a Black woman like you get so much money"? The questions had been highly inappropriate and racially biased. In another instance, Chicago inspectors asked a black woman who worked for United Airlines in Chicago how it was possible that she would travel to Jamaica when she had not worked during the previous month. Despite the fact she provided detailed responses to their questions, while explaining that her live-in boyfriend supported her financially, she was subjected to a pat down while an inspector allegedly picked through her hair (Galbraith, 2001).

This problem is not specific to Chicago's O'Hare airport. In fact, according to legal documents, the director of a customs port in New York issued a memorandum to airport directors, among whom was the director of O'Hare's airport, which stated that unemployed black women were "particularly likely to be drug smugglers" (*Anderson v. Cornejo*). It is obvious that this memorandum enforces the belief that black women are simply suspicious and should be searched since they are, in the mind of this director, likely to engage in illegal activities.

There are stories after stories of individuals being singled out at airports by customs officials, since they simply "fit the profile" of someone considered to be "suspicious." More specifically, there seems to be a disproportionately large number of cases such as the one pertaining to Bosede Adedeji, a Nigerian citizen, who alleged that inspectors never asked her to explain the reasons why she purchased a ticket in cash. Or perhaps they never questioned the reasons for her previous trips, yet they cited reasons related to the fact she bought her ticket in cash and she traveled frequently when justifying their searches on Ms. Adedeji (Galbraith, 2001).

In addition to class and race, the issue of gender also seems to serve as a proxy for criminality by U.S. Customs officials. The Customs' manual seems to train inspectors to be suspicious of women, particularly those married and traveling alone. According to the manual, inspectors are encouraged to "look closely at the jewelry worn on the hands. Is there a wedding ring? If so, where is the spouse?" The manual also justifies treating a solitary woman as a suspect, explaining that "few married people vacation abroad by themselves without being up to something. According to the manual, married women on sightseeing trips without their husbands constitute a high-risk passenger in more ways than one" (Galbraith, 2001).

According to legal scholar Sheri Lynn Johnson, racial profiling still takes place due to the fact there is no sanction against it. The U.S. Supreme Court allows the Immigration and Naturalization Service to utilize ethnic criteria when profiling individuals; thus, one could argue that it allows them to engage in some form of racial profiling. In addition to the Supreme Court allowance for customs to use ethnic factors when predicting someone's criminality, the internal regulations of customs do not prohibit the consideration of racial indicators.

When confronted with these accusations, U.S. Customs officials attempt to minimize the significance of searches or of determining criminality of an individual based on that person's race or ethnic origin. As part of their minimization strategy, they contend that the "pat-downs" are not as invasive and humiliating as it is alleged because they are short in duration. According to documents presented by customs, pat-downs are done on individuals via their outer clothing by an official of the same sex as the subject. In addition, customs officials have often cited improperly trained inspectors as the reason why there is an apparent trend of racial profiling among them (Galbraith, 2001).

It is clear that the terrorist acts of 9/11 have elevated the issue of racial profiling to a different/higher level. Although some erroneously predicted that the racial profiling issue would end as the country was going to focus all of its attention on the war on terror, it is now clear that racial profiling continues to be the point of attention in both political and academic camps across the United States.

HERBERT PACKER'S DUE PROCESS AND CRIME CONTROL MODEL

Perhaps one way to understand the apparent paradigm shift after 9/11 as it relates to racial profiling is to refer to Herbert Packer's Due Process and Crime Control models, introduced in the 1964 University of Pennsylvania Law Review. Specifically, Packer (1964) argued that in every society at a given time, the pendulum of due process and crime control tends to swing in one direction more so than the other. For instance, it could be argued that in the 1960s, in the United States, the pendulum swung to the due process model as emphasis was placed on the rights of the individuals. However, given the tragic events of 9/11, it can be argued that the pendulum has returned to crime control while abandoning due process. This emphasis on crime control seems to disregard the ethical and legal issues relevant to racial profiling. Thus, it seems that the war on terror justifies, in the minds of some, racial and ethnic profiling of individuals.

The issue that has to be contended by all of us is whether or not we wish to live in a society that disregards best practices relating to the treatment of fellow citizens for the sake of feeling protected. The argument that supports racial profiling for the sake of homeland security is simply not strong and holds very little logic. That is, the idea that somehow we will stop the next terrorist attack by engaging in racial profiling toward Muslims or perhaps those that appear to be of Middle Eastern descent is simply not valid. It could be argued that all terrorist groups need to do given this possibility is to pay someone off who appears, for all practical and physical purposes, to be a native of the United States. Thus, our racial profiling initiatives would actually help terrorists in becoming less predictable and more effective in their mission to inflict damage to the United States.

It is very difficult to predict with some degree of accuracy whether or not terrorism will one day cease to exist. Further, it is equally difficult to predict, with some degree of certainty, if the war on terror will end in our lifetime. In all likelihood, it will never cease; further, if we were to win the war on terror, most of us in the United States would not know about it as it is hard to measure success given the complexities of the enemy we fight. Thus, it is feasible that the war on terror and all social implications connected to this, as well as homeland security, will likely continue for years to come. Thus, it is reasonable to expect that racial profiling will continue to be a frequently debated topic during the era of homeland security.

References

Amnesty International (2006). *Threat and Humiliation: Racial Profiling, National Security, and Human Rights in the United States*. New York: Amnesty International USA.

Anderson v. Cornejo, 97 C. 7556 (N.D. Ill. Filed June 24, 1999). *Plaintiffs' Reply Memorandum in Support of Motion to Compel Discovery* at exh. 4.

Begley et al. (2001). "What Price Security?" *Newsweek*. Vol. 138, No. 14.

Corey Dade (2002). "Despite New Guidelines, Fliers Raise Bias Issues." *Boston Globe*, February 2, 2002 at B1.

Detroit Free Press (2001). *Scouts Say They Were Victims of Racial Profiling*. October 17, 2001.

Galbraith, Rayne (Fall, 2001). "Raped by U.S. Customs: Strip Searches and the War on Black Women." Dissertation. University of California at Berkley.

Houston Chronicle (2001). "American Airlines Pilot Removes Arab-American in Secret Service from Plane." December 28, 2001.

Ken Leiser (2002). "Ethnic Profiling at Airports Gains Supporters." St. Louis Post-Dispatch, April 11, 2002.

Norman, Y. Mineta (2001). *Statement Before the U.S. Commission on Civil Rights*. Briefing on Boundaries of Justice: Immigration Policies Post-September 11, October 12, 2001.

Orange County Register (2001). *California Congressman Excluded From Flight by Air France*. Santa Ana, CA. October 31, 2001.

Packer, Herbert (1964). "Two Models of the Criminal Process." University of Pennsylvania Law Review. Vol. 113, No. 1, pp. 1–68.

U.S. Department of Justice (2002). *The USA Patriot Act: Preserving Life and Liberty*. U.S. Government Printing Office: Washington, DC.

CHAPTER 8

Racial Profiling Case Law

Although it is clear, from the previous chapters, that racial profiling is a phenomenon that has affected almost all major aspects of the law enforcement community, its impact has not been limited to the criminal justice system. That is, racial profiling has also affected the legal field generally and case law in particular. To say that there are abundant cases that pertain directly to racial profiling would be to misrepresent the truth. In fact, most criminal and civil cases that in one way or another raise the racial profiling issue derive from a much broader legal issue. For instance, a particular case that pertains to the use of force by police officers may be filed with the courts; however, since the officer may have been Caucasian and the alleged victim, a member of the minority class, racial profiling may be an issue to contend. However, it may not be the central issue of the case as the alleged victim may not be citing racial profiling violations per se. Despite this, most attorneys representing the alleged victim often seek official documents relevant to possible racial tendencies from the law enforcement officer in question. This would be particularly true if the police department or officer would be subject to state law on racial profiling.

In this chapter, we will explore the major cases relevant to racial profiling that have been filed and heard by the U.S. Supreme Court. These cases have established the legal framework for racial profiling-related laws, which have also been challenged in local and federal courts throughout the United States. Thus, they are extremely important and relevant when discussing the legal field's relation to racial profiling.

U.S. SUPREME COURT CASES

Terry v. Ohio

In 1963, a plainclothes police officer, Detective Martin McFadden, who was patrolling his assigned beat, in Cleveland, Ohio, noticed two individuals, Terry and Chilton. The officer had never seen these men before until this particular day. Detective McFadden had developed the habit of looking out for shoplifters and pickpockets during his beat by watching people on the streets. In this particular case, something "did not look right" to the officer so he began to watch the two men closely. He saw one of them walk a relatively short distance and look into a store window. He then walked back to his companion and conferred. The second man then did the same thing as the previous individual. According to Detective McFadden, the two men repeated this action at least five or six times until a third individual, Katz, approached them. When Katz left the two men, they followed soon thereafter (Pampel, 2004).

These particular actions raised the suspicion of officer McFadden as he felt that the men were "casing a job, a stickup" and may have a weapon in their possession. When officer McFadden saw the men in front of the store, he proceeded to confront them by identifying himself as a police officer and asking the men to identify themselves. After the men seemed to "mumble something," officer McFadden proceeded to spin Terry around and patted down the outside of his clothing. Officer McFadden then felt a pistol and ordered the men back in the store, where he removed the pistol from Terry. Once the men were inside the store, the officer patted all of them and found another pistol (which was removed), this time from Chilton. He then took Terry and Chilton to the police station, where he charged them with the act of carrying a concealed weapon.

The case ultimately ended up in court, where Terry and Chilton's attorneys moved to have the evidence related to the pistol removed. They argued that the gun had been discovered during an unlawful search; that is, a search without the officer having probable cause for the arrest. The court rejected the motion entered by Terry and Chilton and the defendants were found guilty. The case was unsuccessfully appealed and both the court of appeals and the Ohio State Supreme Court dismissed it. Ultimately, in 1968, the U.S. Supreme Court considered the case and rendered its opinion, accordingly.

The legal issues considered in this case related to the grounds for search and seizure under the constitutional provisions related to the Fourth Amendment. The central question raised in this case is whether or not it was reasonable to seize and subject an individual to a search without probable cause. The side representing the police argued that Terry was never seized, thus the Fourth Amendment did not apply in this particular case. Specifically, it was argued that a quick frisk of the outside clothing does not constitute a full search. It was further argued that even if the search had involved a seizure, as indicated in the Fourteenth Amendment, it was justified; further, the officer acted in a manner which was required of him to protect himself from the subjects given the suspicious manner in which they were acting.

On the other side, the petitioners claimed that their search involved a seizure. Thus, Terry was restrained from moving around as he pleased, given the actions taken by the officer. According to their argument, the indignity and the threat to personal integrity posed by a search, albeit a brief one, is considered to be serious to the extent that it deserves protection by the Fourth Amendment. It was further argued that the search performed by officer McFadden lacked probable cause or evidence that the suspect had committed a serious crime. Thus, the officer had no authority to perform the search.

It should be noted that the Fourth Amendment to the U.S. Constitution affirms that "the rights of the people to be secure in their persons, houses, papers, and effects, against unreasonable searches and seizures, shall not be violated, and no Warrants shall issue, but upon probable cause, supported by Oath or affirmation, and particularly describing the place to be searched, and the persons or things to be seized" (Findlaw, 2006).

Ultimately, the U.S. Supreme Court heard the Terry appeal and although it was agreed that this particular case raised important constitutional issues, it was rejected. That is, the Court rejected the petition to remove evidence from the trial based on the search. The decision was written by Chief Justice Earl Warren, who stated that whenever practical, police officers must obtain advanced judicial approval in the form of a warrant for all searches and seizures. However, in other instances, on-the-spot observations by the police may require swift action that would not allow enough time to obtain a warrant. For instance, if an officer would have reason to believe that his/her safety and that of others would be compromised, the officer may not be able to wait for the time it would normally take for a judge to issue a warrant. Thus, it is in the government's interest, according to Judge Warren, to adhere to the notion that preventing harm takes place instead of concerns about invading someone's privacy (Pampel, 2004).

This decision and others similar have had the effect of reaffirming the validity of taking action on instances when officers have reasonable suspicion. In other words, police officers need more than just a simple feeling in order to perform a search. Further, they must also limit their actions in order to ensure that they don't take more than the necessary amount of time from suspects. However, critics of this decision affirm that the Court gave police officers too much discretion. In fact, they argue that officers can hide their true intent to racially profile individuals as long as they perform searches allowed by this particular case. For instance, an individual of minority descent can cause suspicion to an officer due to the person's race; however, when confronted with this, the officer may publicly state that the suspect was searched since this individual posed an apparent threat to the security of others.

United States v. Brignoni-Ponce

Another major case involves Brignoni-Ponce. In this case, two U.S. Border Patrol agents were observing traffic traveling away from Mexico as they parked on the side of an interstate highway in California (between San Diego and Los Angeles). The two agents noticed that the occupants of one particular vehicle appeared to be of Mexican descent. The agent pursued the vehicle and eventually ended up stopping it and questioning the passengers. Two of the individuals questioned lacked documentation and had entered the United States illegally. The driver, Brignoni-Ponce, was charged with transporting illegal aliens; he was eventually convicted for these crimes. The trial judge rejected the claim made by the defense that the evidence obtained came from an illegal stop and seizure. However, the court of appeals eventually reversed the earlier conviction, claiming that the stop made by the agents was not based on reasonable suspicion. Thus, the evidence obtained should have been excluded. The U.S. Supreme Court agreed to hear the appeal from the government after the reversal was made (Pampel, 2004).

The Court addressed the question of whether or not a vehicle and occupants can be stopped near the border when the occupants appear to be of Mexican ancestry and this gives reason for suspicion. The government held that it had several grounds that justified the stopping of the vehicle. First, it argued that the Immigration and Naturalization Act authorizes officers to question any individual believed to be an alien about his or her right to be or remain in the United States. Thus, this statute allows the questioning of people who appear to be of Mexican ancestry near the border. In addition, the government argued that another statute grants agents the authority to stop vehicles and question the occupants about their citizenship. This is allowed as long as it takes place within 100 miles of the border.

The U.S. Supreme Court ended up affirming the ruling earlier made by the appellate court. According to the Supreme Court justices, the trial court made the error of allowing introduction of evidence from the stop of Brignoni-Ponce and in convicting the defendant. In addition to determining that the evidence had been obtained in an illegal manner, the Court helped create a standard for making a traffic stop. That is, the decision gave the border control authority to stop vehicles, for a short amount of time, for the purpose of preventing illegal immigration. However, it established that a vehicle cannot be stopped without reason to suspect that the occupants have, in one way or another, violated any laws.

Perhaps one of the most significant contributions of this case is that it established that in order to have reasonable suspicion, agents should consider a number of factors in addition to the individual's ethnic appearance. For instance, information on recent illegal border crossings, experience with immigration traffic in the area, erratic driving, and the use of vans particularly used for smuggling of immigrants should all be considered. In addition, the Court declared that agents may consider other factors such as the individual's haircut and way of dressing, which may indicate that this person lives outside the United States. The Court specifically declared that relying on a specific and single factor, appearing to be of Mexican ancestry, does not meet the standard relevant to reasonable suspicion established in the law.

The last segment of the decision also posed interesting contrasting ideas. That is, the Court declared that "The likelihood that any given person of Mexican ancestry is an alien is high enough to make Mexican appearance a relevant factor, but standing alone does not justify stopping all Mexican-Americans to ask if they are aliens." Although not apparently evident, the Court suggests that ethnic profiling, with some limitations, is within the framework of the U.S. Constitution (Pampel, 2004).

Despite the fact, it is clear that this case establishes that the use of race and ethnicity (or national origin) as sole factors in making a stop violates all major constitutional protections. Even though it could be argued that this case applies specifically to immigration, its implications can reach the scope of racial profiling in drug cases and terrorism. However, it is clear that the decision does not exclude race and ethnicity as a relevant factor in the overall profile of a suspect. One could argue, after reviewing this case, racial profiling remains, according to the Court, a legal practice.

United States v. Sokolow

A major case that merits discussion is *United States v. Sokolow*. In 1984, Andrew Sokolow bought two round-trip airplane tickets to Miami at the Honolulu airport. He purchased these under the names of "Andrew Kray" and "Janet Norian," while paying $2,100 in cash for the tickets. According to the case, Sokolow paid for the tickets from a large roll of $20 bills; he was dressed in a black jumpsuit with a great deal of gold jewelry. Also, he reportedly appeared nervous and did not check in any of the multiple pieces of luggage he and his companion had in their possession. The Honolulu Police Department was alerted of Sokolow's suspicious activity, who in turn alerted the Drug Enforcement Agency (DEA). Upon Sokolow's return to Hawaii a few days later, the DEA sniffing dog alerted authorities of the possibility of drugs in their luggage. As a result, after obtaining a search warrant, the DEA agents found cocaine in the luggage (Pampel, 2004).

Sokolow was charged with possession of cocaine with the intent to distribute, but his legal team filed a motion to suppress the evidence citing that it was illegally obtained. Although the trial judge argued that the agents had reasonable suspicion to search Sokolow's luggage, the appellate judges disagreed, reversing the conviction. The case reached the U.S. Supreme Court, which granted *certiorari* to review the appeals court decision, given the implications of the case. In case you are wondering, *certiorari* is a Latin word which means "to be informed of, or to be made certain in regard to." It is also a name typically given to certain appellate proceedings for reexamination of actions of a trial court, or perhaps even an inferior appeals court (Lawinfo, 2006).

The attorneys representing the government argued that six factors prompted reasonable suspicion in this particular case. These are

1. Cash payment for ticket.
2. Traveling under a name that did not match the given phone number.
3. A destination known as a source of illegal drugs.
4. A stay in Miami for only 48 hours when the round-trip flight took 30 hours.
5. A nervous demeanor.
6. Not checking in luggage.

According to the government attorneys, these characteristics fit the profile of a drug trafficker closely enough to warrant suspicion on behalf of the authorities. Further, the alert prompted by the dog gave the officers probable cause (PC) to open the luggage and subsequently identify the drugs.

The defense team, however, claimed that the search on Sokolow did not meet the standards established by the Fourth Amendment to the U.S. Constitution. Accordingly, the defense team argued that the six factors cited by DEA agents are simply not valid reasons to become suspicious of an individual; that is, these factors also fit the behaviors of a great deal of people who are not necessarily drug traffickers. Thus, in their view, the evidence should be dismissed since it was obtained illegally.

In a 7 to 2 vote, the U.S. Supreme Court ruled in favor of the DEA agents by affirming that they had reasonable suspicion that led to the search of the luggage of Sokolow. According to the Court, since reasonable suspicion carries a minimal level of objective evidence rather than certainty, factors that have been associated with criminality are in fact relevant. In addition, the Court emphasized the importance of relying on a totality of circumstances and not on an individual factor per se to develop enough suspicion to warrant action on their behalf.

Even though this particular case does not focus specifically on racial profiling, it does bring up important points that may, in one way or another, affect the racial profiling issue. For instance, when considering the standard of reasonable suspicion, law enforcement agents do not need to posses suspicion for criminal conduct; rather, they may rely on characteristics which in the past have had some degree of correlation with criminal activity. Although in this case, these characteristics do not include race or ethnicity, given the legality of the use of profiles, it is clear that the Sokolow ruling may allow for the restrictive use of racial profiling. In other words, race and ethnicity could be used as long as these are part of a more general profile.

Michael A. Whren and James L. Brown v. U.S.

Another important case to review is *Whren and Brown* v. *U.S.* In 1993, a police unmarked vehicle in Washington DC observed a Pathfinder truck which seemed to be waiting on a stop sign in an area known for drug usage. The truck was being occupied by young men and bore license plates that were temporary in nature. Further, the truck seemed to remain idle at an intersession for more than 20 seconds—deemed by law enforcement agents as "too much time." When the police turned their unmarked unit around, the truck quickly turned right and sped off at a fast rate. The police then pursued the vehicle alongside until they both stopped. It was then that an officer approached the driver and noticed that one of the passengers had in his possession two bags of cocaine. He then arrested the suspects for possession of illegal drugs (Pampel, 2004).

Once the defendants were charged with violating federal drug laws, they moved to suppress the evidence arguing that the stop and seizure of drugs was illegal. Specifically, they argued that the police did not have probable cause that the passengers had any involvement with drugs. However, these arguments were met by the government's statements which suggested that the police approached the car based on something other than a search for drugs. They had probable cause to stop the car for traffic violations, according to the government attorney. The district court denied the motion to suppress evidence and the suspects were consequently convicted on all counts. The conviction was affirmed by the court of appeals and the case was ultimately heard by the U.S. Supreme Court. The legal issue is based on the use of a traffic stop as a pretext to search for criminality. The government argued that the police was in pursuit of the vehicle due to traffic violations and they simply stumbled on the criminal evidence once they approached the vehicle. The defendants argued that drivers are simply not able to comply with traffic laws all the time; thus, this gives reason (almost all the time) for police to stop any vehicle they wish, under the pretext of a traffic violation.

The U.S. Supreme Court ruled unanimously that the officers did not act unconstitutionally when making the traffic stop. Thus, the evidence they obtained and submitted to the courts was legally seized. The ruling offered by the Court was based on the notion that the fairness of a stop is not dependent on the motive of the officers. That is, according to the Court, attempting to establish whether an officer had the proper state of mind in making a stop would present a difficult, if not impossible task for the court system (Pampel, 2004).

The Court rejected the claim that the legality of a traffic stop should depend on the actions of a reasonable officer in the same circumstances. Further, it also rejected the claim that since traffic laws are so broad, it is difficult to obey these; thus, everyone is guilty of something almost all the time.

The *Whren* decision allows for the legality of the common police strategy of making stops for minor violations a pretext for identifying evidence or some other (more significant) legal activity. For instance, on highways, the police could stop someone for a traffic violation, and then they can check the license plate number, look at the passenger, or view the contents of the vehicle for evidence of a crime. The implications of this case to racial profiling involve the premise that the police could stop someone for racist-related reasons and simply declare the intentions of the officer as having been related to traffic-related violations.

United States v. Armstrong et al.

This particular case took place in 1992, when a California federal district court attorney indicted Christopher Lee Armstrong and other individuals. The indictment was for the charge of conspiring to possess cocaine with the intent to distribute; in addition, it cited violations of federal firearms laws. The charges followed federal and local agents from Inglewood, California, who had obtained information from confidential informants about the defendants' criminal intent. Apparently, the defendants had infiltrated the cocaine distribution ring and made substantial purchases of crack cocaine. Also, they had observed the defendants carry illegal firearms. All of these actions resulted in a sting operation, where the agents videotaped a drug deal, searched for the hotel room where the exchange had taken place, and arrested the suspects, who were found to be in possession of crack cocaine and a loaded gun.

The defendants were African American and filed a motion for discovery or dismissal of their case, arguing that the prosecutors had selected their case due to the fact that they were all minorities. To support their motion, they offered evidence that all of the 24 cases handled in 1991 by the public defender involved African Americans. However, the government opposed the motion stating that the defendants did not provide evidence relevant to the failure of the police to prosecute defendants of races outside African Americans. The motion was granted by the federal court, which ordered the government to allow for discovery; that is, to allow for defendants to receive statistics on the race of the defendants in all drugs and firearms cases over a period of three years. Since the government refused to provide this data, the charges were ultimately dismissed. The court of appeals then reversed the lower district court's decision, resulting in the admission of the case before the U.S. Supreme Court (Pampel, 2004).

The issue at hand pertains to the kind of evidence needed in order to demonstrate racial profiling in prosecution decision making. The defendants, who believed that their investigation and prosecution was based on race, needed data in order to substantiate their claims. However, the government disagreed, stating that instead of race, prosecutors had relied on the large amounts of cocaine relevant to this case, the videotape made of the drug exchange, the defendants' history regarding their involvement with drugs, and the firearms law violation.

The U.S. Supreme Court ruled that the defendants did not demonstrate, in their arguments, that racial profiling had taken place and that therefore there was a need for discovery. In order to establish discrimination based on race, the defendants had to demonstrate that the government had declined to prosecute similar cases involving individuals who were not African Americans. Specifically, the Court argued that without specific information on the circumstances of other cases, the race and ethnicity of the defendants of a case and similar statistics would fall short of demonstrating racial bias. One could argue that this case is very specific to the rules of discovery relevant to race; however, there is much more in this case than simply a quick orientation on the parameters of discovery. The case establishes the criterion that the individual attempting to show discrimination needs to present evidence suggesting that in similar circumstances, other races have been treated differently. In addition, this case establishes that the mere presence of figures on the proportion of minority defendants or of vehicles driven by minority drivers that are subsequently stopped by the police would by themselves not necessarily show that discrimination has taken place. In short, the threshold to demonstrate that in a particular case, racial profiling has taken place is simply narrowed even further.

APPELLATE CASES

All of the cases discussed so far are special in that they have been reviewed by the U.S. Supreme Court. However, most cases heard by federal and state courts never reach the highest court in the land. This, however, does not diminish their importance or relevance to a particular issue. In the case of racial profiling, there are several cases that have reached federal appellate courts. Of these, two seem to be cited the most and have the most relevance to the issue of racial profiling.

UNITED STATES v. *TRAVIS*

The first of these cases is *United States* v. *Travis*. In this case, a detective, in 1992, working in the Cincinnati/Northern Kentucky airport decided to check a flight from Los Angeles. The detective was looking for drug couriers since this particular flight had, in previous instances, produced several drug-related arrests. The detective employed an interesting methodology to identify potential drug dealers. He looked at the list of names on the passenger list trying to identify the ones that sounded like aliases. One particular name, Angel Chavez, seemed suspicious to him since it included a common Hispanic last name with a not so common Hispanic first name (Pampel, 2004).

In the process of obtaining more information on Chavez, the detective found out that she had purchased the flight ticket only a few hours prior to departing; this, according to the detective, is one of the most common practices of drug couriers. The detective ended up making contact with Chavez once she left the plane, at which time he asked her to produce a driver's license and airline ticket. The detective then noticed that the last name on the ticket and that on the license did not match; thus, he obtained permission to search her bag. Upon searching Chavez's bag, the detective found cocaine and proceeded to arrest her.

In the pretrial hearing, the defendant moved to suppress the evidence since, according to her, the detective was discriminatory against her on the basis of her race. Despite this claim, the district court denied the motion to suppress; it was then that Chavez entered a conditional guilty plea. The issue was then considered by the Sixth Circuit Court of Appeals.

It was ultimately decided by the appellate court that the detective had gathered sufficient information before the contact was made in order to justify approaching Chavez. According to the court, the fact that the detective did not make contact with other Hispanics on board the plane in spite of the presence of other issues that raised concern (i.e., one-way ticket being purchased a few hours before departing) makes it clear that the officer was not specifically singling out an individual based on race or ethnicity. The implication of this case is that solely relying on race is not allowed; however, using race along with other descriptors is allowed and permissible under the law.

United States v. Montero-Camargo et al.

Another important case to consider is *United States* v. *Montero-Camargo et al.* In this case, the defendants, German Espinoza Montero-Camargo and Lorenzo Sanchez-Guillen, were driving two different cars on a highway in California (near the border). Both cars made U-turns and the authorities were alerted of this. Once federal agents arrived at the scene, they noticed two cars stopped at a location known for being a pick-up site for illegal aliens. As the agents neared the car, they noticed that the individuals occupying the vehicles were Hispanic, which furthered their suspicion (Pampel, 2004).

After detaining the passengers, the agents proceeded to search the trunk, where they found two large bags of marijuana. All passengers were charged with possession of marijuana with the intent to distribute. In response, the defendants filed a pretrial motion to suppress the evidence based on the grounds that agents did not have reasonable suspicion to initiate the stop. The district court denied the motion to suppress, which prompted the defendants to file an appeal.

The main legal issue in this case centered on the question of whether the Border Patrol agents had substantial suspicion to stop Montero-Camargo. The government argued that numerous factors, including the Mexican license plates on the vehicles, the U-turn, and the location where the vehicles were parked, contributed to the suspicion held by the agents. However, the defense team disagreed, claiming that making a U-turn and stopping at a highway do not constitute grounds for suspicion. Accordingly, it was argued that the patrol agents violated the defendants' rights against unreasonable search and seizure.

The Ninth Circuit Court of Appeals affirmed the lower court's decision on the issue of the legality of the stop. However, in doing so, the Court also declared that the agents had used inappropriate criteria in holding suspicion. Accordingly, making a U-turn and stopping at a location where illegal activity occurs constitute reasonable suspicion; however, being of Hispanic appearance, does not.

Although the case has very little impact on Border Patrol agents, it potentially has a great deal of importance with regard to the use of race and ethnicity when determining suspicion. The circuit judge Reinhardt's opinion on this case was that the *Brignoni-Ponce* case (where race and ethnicity were deemed as appropriate when determining reasonable suspicion) was "handed down in 1975, some 25 years ago. Current demographic data demonstrate that the statistical premises on which the dictum relies are no longer applicable" (Pampel, 2004). That is, due to the large number of Hispanics in the general population, the previous argument that race and ethnicity could be used as supporting ground for reasonable suspicion is no longer valid. The case falls short of outlawing the use of race and ethnicity but it provokes questions which may end up being resolved by the U.S. Supreme Court at a later date.

STATE COURT CASES

Although many state courts have considered the issue of racial profiling, there are two particular states, Maryland and New Jersey, that have seen most of the action in their court systems with regard to this issue. The courts in these states have heard three of the most important cases relevant to the racial profiling issue. These will be discussed in some detail.

Wilkins v. Maryland State Police

The first of these cases, *Wilkins v. Maryland State Police*, related to Robert L. Wilkins, a black, Washington DC, criminal defense attorney, who was traveling with family members late at night on a highway close to Cumberland, Maryland. A state trooper from Maryland stopped the car and expressed his desire to search the car. Having identified himself as an attorney, Wilkins refused to allow the trooper to search the vehicle. However, the officer then mentioned that he would have to wait for the drug-sniffing dogs to check the car. When the dogs arrived, the passengers were forced to get out of the car into the rain. Nothing was found and Wilkins was issued a citation for speeding. In turn, Wilkins decided to take legal action and gathered support from several civil rights groups, including the ACLU. The lawsuit represented Wilkins and other minority members who had been treated similarly.

The basis of the lawsuit included the argument that the Maryland State Police had violated the Fourteenth Amendment when using racial characteristics. As part of the legal process, the plaintiffs received a report from the Maryland State Police which referred to the fact that troopers had been given specific information relevant to black drug couriers who were traveling through Maryland in rental cars with Virginia license plates. A statistical report produced by an expert hired by the defendants suggested that there were few differences in speeding by race but significant differences in stops made by the police.

All parties involved in the lawsuit agreed to a settlement. This included damages of $50,000 for the occupants of the cars and $46,000 in attorney's fees. More significantly, it required the Maryland State Police to abstain from using racial-based drug courier profiles in stopping, detaining, or searching motorists; train all officers on the policy; maintain records of race-related stops and searches; and discipline officers who violate the policy on racial profiling. The settlement also specified the manner in which performance was going to be measured.

This case is highly significant as it was the first one of its kind to show state-based action against racial profiling. However, it did not produce a legal precedence as the state of Maryland banned racial profiling before the settlement occurred.

New Jersey v. Pedro Soto et al.

In New Jersey, 17 defendants of African American descent who had been subject to a traffic stop and subsequently arrested on the turnpike, between 1988 and 1991, filed a lawsuit against the New Jersey State Police. They complained that the New Jersey State Police practiced discriminatory enforcement of the law and suppressed the evidence. The importance of this case is that the claim made relied on statistical data that showed disparity in stops and arrests of minority drivers (Pampel, 2004).

The defendants cited several facts that served as evidence to support their claim. One of these was a study that showed that the percentage of stops of black drivers on highways was greater than the percentage of black drivers who sped. The second study filed compared speeding tickets based on the use of radar with speeding tickets based on the observation by officers. The findings produced in this study suggested that minorities received tickets less often when the observation was by radar rather than by police officers. The point here is that when police discretion was removed (radar-based tickets), minorities received fewer tickets. This shows, according to the defendants, that minorities were being targeted by state troopers. The final piece of evidence submitted by the defendants came in the form of two state troopers who testified that they had been trained and coached to make profile stops in an attempt to interdict the transportation of drugs.

When comparing the evidence submitted by the defendants with the expert testimony filed by the state police that refuted the claims of the studies referenced earlier, it was clear to the judge that the defense's statistical evidence was more credible. Thus, the judge stated that the state must introduce specific evidence that shows that "there are actually defects which bias the results or the missing factors, when properly organized and accounted for, eliminate or explain the disparity" (Pampel, 2004). The ruling concluded that the facts presented showed, in a clear manner, that the state police leaders failed to monitor or supervise efforts to stop drug trafficking; in so doing, the police continued to discriminate against African Americans by racially profiling them.

The significance of this case is that it relied heavily on statistical evidence in order to demonstrate racial profiling. This legitimizes, to some extent, before the courts, the use of statistical measures to show disparity in the individuals stopped, searched, and arrested by the police. The decision in this case led to the dismissal of charges against 17 defendants along with 100 other minority defendants arrested on the New Jersey highway. It also led to changes in police procedures and a settlement with the Department of Justice that allowed for federal government representatives to supervise efforts to eliminate use of race profiling in highway contacts.

Peso Chavez et al. v. Illinois State Police

This particular case involves a Hispanic private investigator who was hired by a defense attorney to obtain information on police behavior. The plan was for Chavez to travel several times through an Illinois highway and for someone to follow him in order to observe police behavior. In one instance, a state trooper followed Chavez and stopped him after determining that the car driven by Chavez was rented. According to the trooper, Chavez had used air freshener, had maps open inside the car, and was acting nervously. The officer issued a warning ticket and after doing so, asked Chavez if he could search the vehicle. Chavez refused, indicating he had to leave as soon as possible. However, the trooper asked for drug-sniffing dogs, which arrived about 35 to 55 minutes later. They did not find drugs and Chavez was eventually allowed to leave. This particular incident led Chavez to file a class-action suit in 1994. In it, he claimed that the search he was subject to originated from racial profiling, and further, that it violated his civil rights. The case was dismissed but was later considered for appeal.

Under the current standard, a claim of discrimination must show that the defendant's actions contained a discriminatory effect and were motivated by an intent that was also discriminatory in nature. However, after the appellate court heard the case, it dismissed it agreeing with the lower court decision. Specifically, the court indicated that the plaintiff did not prove that the officers of the Illinois State Police stop, detain, and search African American and Hispanic motorists disproportionately as a mechanism of racial profiling. Further, the court identified flaws in the statistics that made these inadequate and not appropriate for this case. This particular case showed that the statistics have to demonstrate that minorities would have been treated differently if found in similar circumstances as their Caucasian counterparts. Further, they have to be relevant to the case in that they must demonstrate disparity toward minorities.

The significance of these cases with respect to racial profiling is clear. They not only show the relevance and timeliness of the topic but they also serve as evidence that racial profiling is a concept that is fast advancing in the court system. Thus, at some point, it is our hope that racial profiling will be defined and conceptualized in such a manner that it will be clear, to criminal justice practitioners and researchers alike, what the legal threshhold is regarding racial profiling. Until then, we can only hope that the courts in general and the U.S. Supreme Court specifically will define and establish a legal norm with which racial profiling can be conceptualized.

References

Findlaw (2006). http://caselaw.lp.findlaw.com/data/constitution/amendment14/

Lawinfo (2006). http://www.lawinfo.com/index.cfm/fuseaction/Client.lawarea/categoryid/
    1135

Michael A. Whren and James L. Brown v. *United States*, 95-5841 (1995).

New Jersey v. *Pedro Soto* et al., 324 (1996). N.J. Superior Court.

Pampel, Fred C. (2004). Racial Profiling. New York, NY: Facts of Life, Inc.

Peso Chavez et al. v. *Illinois State Police*, 99-3691 (2001). Seventh Circuit Court of Appeals.

Terry v. *Ohio*, 392 U.S. 1 (1968).

United States v. *Armstrong* et al., 95-157 (1996).

United States v. *Brignoni-Ponce*, 422 U.S. 873 (1975).

United States v. *Montero-Camargo* et al., 97-50643 (2000). Ninth Circuit Court of Appeals.

United States v. *Sokolow*, 87-1295 (1989).

United States v. *Travis*, 94-5771 (1995). Sixth Circuit Court of Appeals.

Wilkins v. *Maryland State Police*, 93-468 (1996). District Court of Maryland.

CHAPTER 9

States Respond to Racial Profiling

As of this writing, racial profiling laws have been enacted and are in place in 28 of the 50 states in the United States. It is clear, after reviewing national trends, that it is a matter of time before the remaining states enact racial profiling laws. It is important to review the legislation of those states that are required to record and report racial profiling data. In doing so, note that each state is different with regard to the manner in which data is required to be collected and reported. As you will notice relatively soon into the discussion, racial profiling laws are passed by legislators with the intent of detecting if racial profiling is taking place—they don't aim at recording the intent of the officer when making a traffic stop. Instead, they record the outcome of a traffic stop while controlling for the driver's race and ethnicity. It should be noted that the federal government's initiative to "end racial profiling" made an impact on some of the states by encouraging them to introduce and consequently pass legislation that identifies and endsprofiling practices. The states in the United States that currently have in place racial profiling laws are as follows:

Arkansas	Kansas	Missouri	Oklahoma	Utah
California	Kentucky	Montana	Oregon	Virginia
Colorado	Louisiana	Nebraska	Rhode Island	Washington
Connecticut	Maryland	Nevada	South Dakota	West Virginia
Florida	Massachusetts	New Jersey	Tennessee	
Illinois	Minnesota	North Carolina	Texas	

STATE LAW REQUIREMENTS

Although each state varies with respect to specific requirements for law enforcement agencies, almost all of them focus their attention on traffic-related stops. Further, they also seem to emphasize searches and arrests that stem from contacts between the police and citizens. One major difference relates to the manner in which the data is mandated to be reported. That is, some states require the data to be submitted to a state repository, while others simply ask that each agency submit the data to their own governing body. For the most part, these represent city councils. It is worth examining each of these states with respect to the requirements on data collection and reporting. Most of the information presented derives, primarily, from two sources: the Northeastern University's Institute on Race and Justice and the Police Foundation's publication *Racial Profiling: The State of the Law*.

Arkansas

Background

In 2001, Arkansas state representative Lendell introduced and tried to pass a bill that would require state troopers to record data on each traffic stop. After the bill was withdrawn by its author, the State House Public Transportation Committee voted to study whether the Arkansas State Police practiced racial profiling. The committee felt that the provisions of the proposed bill were not feasible due to the high cost of processing the information across state agencies.

In 2003, the Arkansas legislature passed an act, sponsored by Henry Wilkins, which prompted the creation of a racial profiling task force. In addition, the act mandated policy and training requirements for banning racial profiling among all law enforcement agencies in the state.

Requirements

No data collection required.

California

Background

In 1999, the California legislature successfully passed a bill (SB 78) that required law enforcement agencies to collect traffic-stop data in order to determine if police stopped minorities at disproportionate rates. However, Governor Gray Davis vetoed the legislation. Currently, a large number of jurisdictions in the state are collecting data on a voluntary basis, as part of court settlements or through federal consent decrees.

Requirements

No data collection required.

Colorado

Background

The legislature in the state of Colorado approved House Bill 1114, which mandated data collection by certain law enforcement agencies effective June 5, 2001. The bill requires the Colorado State Patrol and Denver agencies to collect data in instances when officers issue a citation or a warning during the course of a traffic stop.

Requirements

The collection of data relevant to age, race, gender, ethnicity, number of passengers, reason for stop, alleged violation, date, time, location, warning given, citation issued, arrest made, personal search conducted, vehicle search conducted, type of search, contraband found, items captured for forfeiture, and authority for search.

Connecticut

Background

In June 1999, the Connecticut General Assembly signed into law the Act Concerning Traffic Stop Statistics (Public Act No. 99–198). The statute prohibits the state police, municipal police departments, and all other law enforcement agencies in the state from engaging in racial profiling. Furthermore, the act requires the collection of traffic-stop data by state and local police, while establishing a process for investigating citizen complaints on racial profiling. Specifically, each agency must collect traffic-stop data and submit it to the Chief State's Attorney, who is responsible for the analysis of the data and subsequent submission to the governor and the state's General Assembly. The statute was due to expire in 2001 but has been extended since.

Requirements

The law requires the collection of data relevant to age, race, color, gender, ethnicity, reason for stop, alleged violation, date action taken, warning and citation issued, arrest made, personal search performed, and vehicle search conducted.

Florida

Background

In 2002, the Florida House and State introduced bills that were to create the Florida Motorist Task Force, while prescribing the responses of the Attorney General of Florida when a complaint based on racial profiling is filed. Both bills died in committees in March 2002. However, in June 2001, Governor Jeb Bush signed into law Florida Senate Bill 84, which mandates that law enforcement officers throughout the state receive instruction on interpersonal skills relevant to diverse populations and discriminatory profiling. Further, the law also mandates that sheriffs and municipal law enforcement agencies incorporate policies that are antiracial and antidiscriminatory, and provide guidelines and requirements for such policies along with an effective date.

Requirements

No traffic-stop data requirements in place.

Illinois

Background

On July 18, 2003, Governor Rod Blagojevich launched a four-year study on traffic stops as he signed into law Senate Bill 30. Although there were previous attempts to pass legislature relevant to racial profiling, they were not successful. The Illinois Department of

Transportation (IDOT) has assumed responsibility for analyzing the data and releasing its findings each year between July 2005 and July 2007. If the state finds evidence that racial profiling is taking place, the director of the Illinois State Police would implement the appropriate changes in order to modify police procedures and policies.

Requirements

Recording the name, address, gender, and race of motorists stopped by the police. Further, recording if a search was conducted. This requirement was in place until 2007.

Kansas

Background

On February 23, 2005, the Kansas legislature passed House Bill 2683. This particular bill requires all Kansas law enforcement agencies to record and report data on all traffic and pedestrian stops. Specifically, the bill creates a task force with the aim of designing a uniform method of collecting data for statewide use. The bill also defines racial profiling and creates civil remedies for racial profiling victims. Disciplinary guidelines for officers found to engage in racial profiling are also found in the bill.

Requirements

Collection and reporting of data on all traffic-related contacts, including pedestrian stops.

Kentucky

Background

On March 20, 2001, Kentucky governor Paul Patton issued an executive order banning racial profiling in all state police departments. Further, Governor Patton commissioned a study on the race and gender of motorists stopped by the police. A total of 25 local police departments volunteered to participate in the study. The executive order also specified that a model policy should be drafted and distributed to individual agencies for their adoption.

Requirements

No data collection required. However, law requires state agencies to forbid racial profiling and implement written policies.

Louisiana

Background

On June 22, 2001, the state of Louisiana enacted House Bill 1855, which requires all police agencies in the state to collect and report data on traffic-related stops. Exception was made to approximately 13 agencies that had, at the time the bill was enacted, in place policies against racial profiling. In spite of the exemption, some agencies opted to collect and report data as specified by the law. All agencies required to submit the data are to send the information to the Department of Safety on a quarterly basis. This state agency is then required to report the data analysis to the governor and legislature on an annual basis.

Requirements

Collection and reporting of data relevant to age, race, gender, number of passengers, reason for stop, alleged violation, warning or citation issued, arrest made, personal or vehicle search conducted, and type of search performed on a suspect.

Maryland

Background

On April 4, 2001, the state of Maryland enacted legislation that requires law enforcement agencies throughout the state to collect racial profiling data. The statute requires the collection of data by large police departments while gradually adding small departments until 2004. It was then that all jurisdictions, regardless of size, were required to collect racial profiling data until January 1, 2007. The Montgomery County Sheriff Department is the only jurisdiction in Maryland that started collecting data under a Department of Justice consent decree.

Requirements

The Maryland law requires the collection of traffic-contact data relevant to race, gender, ethnicity, reason for stop, alleged violation, date, time, and location of the stop, warning and citation issued, arrest made, personal search conducted, vehicle search conducted, contraband found (if any), items seized, and authority for the search.

Massachusetts

Background

The law requires the state's executive office of Public Safety to work with the Department of State Police and municipal police departments to ensure that adequate efforts are made to identify and eliminate any instances of racial profiling. In addition to requirements relevant to data collection, the law provides for in-service training and a campaign aimed at increasing public awareness on racial and gender profiling. A hotline was also created to facilitate the submission of racial profiling complaints.

Requirements

The law requires the collection and reporting of traffic contact data relevant to race, gender, action taken, warning and citation issued, arrest made, personal or vehicle search performed, and contraband found.

Minnesota

Background

On July 1, 2001, the legislature in Minnesota passed a law establishing voluntary data collection while authorizing a statewide study on racial profiling. The legislation also authorized the allocation of funds to install video cameras in police vehicles of departments that opted to participate in this study. The city of Minneapolis and 67 additional jurisdictions expressed their desire to participate in the data collection campaign.

Requirements

Data collection is voluntary. However, for those agencies participating in the statewide data collection program, information on traffic stops is required. Particularly, this information includes age, race, gender, ethnicity, reason for stop, alleged violation, date, time, location, unit identification, warning and citation issued, arrest made, personal search performed, vehicle search, contraband found (if any), and authority for search.

Missouri

Background

State law (Section 590.650) requires all law enforcement agencies to record and report data relevant to the race of all drivers involved in a traffic stop, search, and arrest. The data is submitted to the Missouri Attorney General's Office annually. Once submitted, the data is compiled in a report submitted to the governor and General Assembly by June 1 of each year. Recently, the state penalized, by withholding funds, law enforcement agencies that did not comply with this mandate.

Requirements

The data required includes age, race, gender, ethnicity, reason for stop, alleged violation, warning or citation issued, arrest made, personal and vehicle search conducted, contraband found, and authority for search.

Montana

Background

The state of Montana enacted a bill in 2003 which defines and prohibits racial profiling. Further, the bill requires law enforcement agencies throughout the state to adopt policies against racial profiling. However, it does not require the collection or reporting of racial profiling data. A bill that would have required this failed passage before the state legislature in 2001.

Requirements

Jurisdictions are not required to collect or report racial profiling data. However, state bans racial profiling and outlines methods of handling citizen complaints. Further, it requires agencies to define elements of racial profiling in the form of a policy.

Nebraska

Background

On May 2001, the Nebraska legislature passed a law prohibiting racial profiling. Further, it required state patrol and local law enforcement agencies to collect and report data on every traffic stop regardless of whether or not a citation or warning is issued. Prior to this, the state patrol had been collecting data on a voluntary basis. According to the law, the submission of data should be performed annually in the form of summary reports to the Nebraska Commission on Law Enforcement and Criminal Justice. The commission may review the data and any allegation that racial profiling has taken place.

Requirements

Data relevant to race, ethnicity, reason for stop, alleged violation, warning or citation issued, arrest made, personal search performed, and vehicle search performed is required.

Nevada

Background

The Nevada legislature passed a bill requiring data collection on all traffic stops by the Nevada Highway Patrol and in all cities whose population is more than 100,000. Through the legislation, a total of nine jurisdictions are participating in this program, in addition to one particular site that is voluntarily collecting data.

Requirements

Collection and reporting of data related to age, race, gender, ethnicity, number of passengers, reason for stop, alleged violation, warning and citation issued, arrest made, personal and vehicle search performed, type of search, items seized and, authority for search.

New Jersey

Background

On March 14, 2003, New Jersey governor James McGreevy signed into law the criminalization of racial profiling, that is, racial profiling by police is considered to be a felony. In addition, the law states that racial discrimination is a violation of civil rights and is subject to imposition of fines and/or imprisonment. The New Jersey Attorney General's Office of Public Integrity is in charge of reviewing complaints against police officers or other public officials. Further, this office has the authority to prosecute or dismiss cases after an investigation has been conducted.

Requirements

Current state law does not require the collection and reporting of traffic contact data. However, the state has been subject to federal intervention that has, from time to time, required agencies to report data on traffic stops and searches for purposes of analysis.

North Carolina

Background

State Senate Bill 76 requires state law enforcement agencies to collect data on the race of individuals stopped. Further, the state's Division of Criminal Statistics is required to collect and analyze the data reported by police departments. Pending legislation, if passed, will require all law enforcement agencies to collect and report data relevant to traffic stops.

Requirements

Current law requires state agencies (only) to record and report traffic-stop data to the Division of Criminal Statistics. All participating agencies are required to verify with the suspect being stopped that the recorded race and/or ethnicity information is accurate. That is, suspect is asked for his/her race and ethnic background.

Oklahoma

Background

In 2000, the Oklahoma state legislature enacted a statute that prohibited racial profiling. The statute mandates only the enactment of racial profiling policies among all law enforcement agencies.

Requirements

State law does not require the collection of traffic data.

Oregon

Background

In June 2001, the Oregon legislature adopted Senate Bill 415, which encourages police departments to collect data relevant to traffic stops. It also creates a law enforcement–contact policy and data review committee to provide assistance to law enforcement agencies. The assistance provided relates to the collection and analysis of data, as well as the dissemination of procedures and policies of jurisdictions that have made progress toward the reduction or elimination of racial profiling.

Requirements

The collection of data relevant to traffic stops is voluntary but strongly encouraged. Participating agencies are asked to record traffic information relevant to age, race, gender, national origin, reason for stop, alleged violation, warning or citation issued, arrest made, and personal or vehicle search performed.

Rhode Island

Background

On July 13, 2000, the Traffic Stops Statistics Act was enacted in the state of Rhode Island. The act bans racial profiling and requires that all state and local police departments collect and report traffic-related data. It also authorizes for the legal redress of people who claim to have been victimized by racial profiling.

Requirements

All local and state law enforcement agencies are required to collect and report traffic-stop data. Information on race, gender, ethnicity, reason for stop, alleged violation, date, time, location, license plate number, warning or citation issued, arrest made, personal or vehicle search performed, contraband found (if any), items seized for forfeiture, and authority for search is required.

South Dakota

Background

Although the notion that law enforcement agencies should be required to record and report the race of drivers during routine traffic stops widely prevails, the state encourages law enforcement agencies to purchase video cameras and install these in police vehicles in an attempt to reduce racial profiling incidents.

Requirements

No state law requiring the collection and reporting of traffic-contact data. However, a state law was passed which encourages law enforcement agencies to purchase and use video cameras in police vehicles.

Tennessee

Background

In February 2005, the state legislature considered House Bill 1925, which would require tracking the ethnic and racial characteristics of people stopped by highway troopers. Similar legislation was defeated earlier, although in 2001, the legislature approved a pilot project in which several law enforcement agencies would record the race of the people stopped by the police. Currently, state law requires the collection and reporting of racial profiling data exclusively by state police.

Requirements

Data collection requirements for state police include information on age, race, color, gender, ethnicity, number of passengers, reasons for stop, alleged violation, citation issued, arrest made, personal and vehicle search conducted, type of search, contraband found, items seized, warrant issued, and authority for search.

Texas

Background

In May 2001, Senate Bill 1074 was passed to become effective January 1, 2002. The law mandated the recording and reporting, by all law enforcement agencies in Texas, of Tier 1 data. This involved recording information about all individuals who come in contact with police in the process of a traffic stop where a citation is issued or arrest is made. Tier 2 data, which is data collected regarding all contacts made with citizens including pedestrians, is required of agencies who did not apply to the state for funds to purchase video cameras. Also, agencies that have video equipment are exempt from the Tier 2 requirement.

Requirements

Traffic-contact information relevant to race, ethnicity, searches performed, types of search, and arrest is required of all agencies in the state. In addition, if the agency did not apply for funds to purchase video equipment or if they don't have video cameras in vehicles, they are required to collect additional information relevant to gender, pedestrian contacts, hazardous versus nonhazardous contacts, outcome of searches, contraband found, type of contraband seized, location of stop, type of contact, and authority for search.

Utah

Background

On March 2002, the legislature passed House Bill 0101, which required racial composition be included on the state's driver's license application. Further, the act also required law enforcement agencies in the state to establish written policies prohibiting unconstitutional traffic enforcement, while mandating the creation of a central database for monitoring traffic- and pedestrian-related stops initiated by law enforcement officers.

Requirements

No data collection requirements are in place although a few law enforcement agencies are participating in voluntary collection of racial profiling data. However, state law mandates that all law enforcement agencies establish policies against racial profiling.

Virginia

Background

Senate Bill 280, which was introduced during Virginia's 2002 legislative session, requires that all local and state law enforcement agencies collect and report data on all traffic stops. Further, this information is to be relayed to the superintendent of police, who is responsible for reporting, on an annual basis, the findings relevant to the data set directly to the governor.

Requirements

Race and related factors are to be recorded and reported by all police agencies in the state.

Washington

Background

On March 2002, the state legislature passed a bill that requires the Washington State Police to collect and report data on each routine traffic stop made regardless of whether or not a citation was issued. The bill also contained language ordering the Washington Association of Sheriffs and Police Chiefs to encourage local law enforcement agencies to voluntarily collect data. As a result, only four jurisdictions agreed to collect data.

An additional bill passed by the state legislature requires that all law enforcement agencies enact policies against racial profiling, while providing additional training for police officers in this regard.

Requirements

No mandate requiring agencies to collect and report data expect for the Washington State Police.

West Virginia

Background

On March 7, 2002,the state of West Virginia passed a law that prohibits law enforcement officers from using race, ethnicity, or national origin when identifying the individuals who will be subject to traffic stops, frisks, questioning, or searches. This law also mandates that state and local law enforcement agencies develop and maintain procedures for receiving, investigating, and responding to allegations relevant to racial profiling. However, the law does not require the collection and reporting of racial profiling data. Only one state agency requires that its officers record race-related data about motorists who are issued citations or are arrested, and also note if force is used.

Requirements

The state does not require the collection of race profiling data.

It is clear, after reviewing racial profiling legislation and its requirements in 28 states across the United States, that each jurisdiction differs in its requirements regarding traffic-contact information. While some require that all contacts are recorded, others are only specific to traffic-related contacts where a citation is issued or an arrest is made. It is clear, however, that many states require the implementation of a racial profiling policy aimed at making it illegal to target individuals based on race or ethnicity. Also, it is evident that multiple states have established a repository of information which is hosted, in most instances, by a state agency.

The point worth considering here is that all of the states considered to be proactive are relying, to a certain degree, on traffic data in order to determine the current state of racial profiling practices. I am not sure that we should agree with this approach, considering the fact that traffic data is only one of the multiple components that may serve as evidence of racial profiling. Further, the data on racial profiling being collected by most states is institutional-level data. This means that this data pertains to the activities of all members of a police department during a given time period. Thus, this is inadequate and simply not useful when considering that racial profiling incidents are typically caused by an individual and not by institutions. Thus, macro-level data is difficult to apply to micro-level situations.

Despite these limitations, it is noteworthy that some states have considered racism in general and racial profiling specifically to be of enough importance to enact legislation regarding the abolition of this practice. Further, it is almost equally impressive that in some cases, a few law enforcement agencies have volunteered to collect and report data absent a state requirement. It is reasonable to expect that in the near future all states in the United States will address, in one form or another, racial profiling by law enforcement officers. Perhaps those states that have had in place, for some time, laws and data collection requirements relevant to racial profiling will serve as role models for others to imitate as they attempt to significantly reduce incidents of racial profiling.

References

Northeastern University's Institute on Race and Justice (2006). *Legislation and Litigation*. Boston, MA: Data Collection Resource Center. http://www.racialprofilinganalysis.neu.edu/legislation/

Police Foundation (2005). *Racial Profiling: The State of the Law*. March 2005.

CHAPTER 10

The Future of the Racial Profiling Paradigm

In this chapter, we will discuss different aspects pertaining to the future of racial profiling. Specifically, we will discuss the specific issues affecting regarding racial profiling and perceptions this concept, the challenges regarding it in the era of Homeland Security, and the future of the racial profiling paradox.

WHY PROFILING?

Of all the social issues that have emerged in the past few years, racial profiling seems to be the one that has caught the public eye most often. Perhaps this is due to the fact that this issue has a visual component that most people have, at some point in their lives, seen. For example, images of Rodney King being beaten by police officers in Los Angeles are still vivid in the minds of many people. It could also be that racial profiling has caught the interest of the public due to the fact that it is an extension of the civil rights struggle in modern times. Thus, many of the people who may be too young to remember the civil rights movement have found in racial profiling the continuation of the struggle to promote equal rights. Also, throughout the United States, racial profiling has found an echo in legislative bodies, whose aim is to promote social justice. To many legislators and related public officials, racial profiling has become an avenue where they can express their support for civil rights. It has also become an avenue to impact the minority community, who have, in recent years, become a strong voting block.

Despite the fact racial profiling has found interest among all of these groups, it is clear that very few (if any) have asked the honest question of how to determine if racial profiling exists. Very few people have quietly removed themselves from external influences to ponder if in fact we can measure racial profiling in a scientific manner. The apparent lack of interest in the genuine research approach toward racial profiling has resulted in legislation (in some cases) where racial profiling is simply not measured properly.

For law enforcement officers, racial profiling has meant a new problem and an endless battle that has no clear victor. Clearly, there are law enforcement agencies throughout the country that are in grave need of collecting racial profiling data specifically for the purpose of providing it to the community to prove their sense of accountability. These police departments have been subject to public attention due to the lack of ethical and professional conduct of their officers. However, those departments that seem to have a pervasive problem related to ethics and legal behavior are only a few. That is, the majority of police officers and police departments in the United States are are honest and hard working. Thus, racial profiling, although occurring from time to time, is not the main problem or challenge affecting these agencies. Despite this, they too are subject to the collection and reporting of racial profiling data. You may wonder what is the harm to a particular law enforcement agency if they are asked to collect data (assuming this agency is law abiding and its officers are ethical and properly training their subordinates)? The answer to this question is simple. Agencies that are subject to racial profiling laws, for the most part, express a feeling of frustration as they realize that they are required to collect and report data since there is a great deal of mistrust among the public. To most police officers, the realization that the public does not trust them is simply devastating. Some have joined the force influenced by the ideals of protecting and serving; thus, they cannot understand why some members of society don't hold them in high regard.

Also, to academics, the issue of racial profiling has presented a new challenge in research. That is, criminologists, whose interest has always lain on race and crime, have found that racial profiling is a tangible entity which encompasses most of the issues studied in the traditional race and crime literature. However, there is some degree of frustration among those of us who study the complexities related to racial profiling. For instance, the notion that data has a limited role when studying this issue is not hard for academics to understand but it seems to be a very difficult topic to discuss with individuals who, regardless of their limited knowledge on data, seem impressed with numbers. Thus, some academics seem to be under pressure to dictate one way or another whether profiling is taken place after reviewing data. Others, however, feel that it is our obligation to preserve the integrity of statistical results and academia; thus, we tend to agree with the opinion that data is limited in nature but does make a contribution to the racial profiling debate.

DISSECTING RACIAL PROFILING

It is difficult to imagine that some people obtain all their information from newspapers and feel that these are credible sources which often tell the truth. This makes it easier for newspaper reporters and other news outlets to appear credible to a receptive audience when publishing results relying on traffic data. While I was visiting the city of San Antonio (Texas) a cabdriver (who happened to be Latina) mentioned to me, as we were leaving the airport on my way to my hotel, that racial profiling was a "very serious problem" in San Antonio. When I asked her from where she obtained this information, she quickly referred to newspaper headlines of the day, which apparently suggested that data just released indicated that racial profiling was taking place in San Antonio. I pressed on and asked her if she really believed that this phenomenon was indeed true. She then made a pause and said that she knew, from a personal standpoint, that racial profiling was a problem in the city of San Antonio since she had been stopped twice by police officers within a few months and that she knew she had been singled out since she was Hispanic. I then went ahead and asked her if she was saying that Hispanic officers singled out Hispanic drivers, indicating to her that a large percentage of officers working for the San Antonio Police Department were Hispanic. She looked astonished and simply abandoned the conversation quickly while recognizing that perhaps she had made a mistake in making these generalities without concrete scientific foundation.

Unfortunately, this particular cabdriver is not alone. Many people today seem to have an opinion about racial profiling based on popular literature themes which are often backed up by data that is either meaningless or has a limited function. Most of the data collected for purposes of racial profiling reporting is based on traffic stops. Thus, this data only shows who is stopped for traffic violations but not the intent of the officer when making the stop. The flawed logic of using traffic stops to determine racial profiling is analogical to any of us making the point that because someone looks muscular it must be that they spend a great deal of time at the gym. Well, the fact that the person is muscular does not necessarily mean that he/she spends any time at the gym. It could be that the person was simply born with an impressive physique or perhaps that the person worked out but not necessarily at a gym. Thus, we cannot say with any degree of certainty that just because 60 more blacks or Hispanics were issued a citation, this must mean that officers are racist. It could be that officers were doing their job in enforcing the law and it just happens to be the case that blacks and Hispanics were issued more citations (due to driving habits or other related issues).

The other item to consider has to do with the notion that, as stated earlier, racial profiling is for the most part an individual-based phenomenon and not an institutional one. Thus, it is hard to imagine an entire law enforcement agency engaging in institutional racism toward all minority drivers. Although it is possible, this is highly unlikely as professional standards and a great deal of oversight on police departments now exists. Thus, aggregate data on the department's overall traffic citations for an entire year falls short of reporting individual-based biases expressed by particular officers. In fact, it is likely that if one or two racist officers work for a police department, the aggregate data for these two racist officers would be hidden and somewhat diluted in the overall data reported, thus making it more difficult to identify and address individual-based racism. Clearly then, just the exercise of collecting and reporting aggregate data is an incomplete effort. It needs to be accompanied by individual-based data—in addition to factors that, when analyzed, may suggest individual-based racism—in order to be meaningful.

IN THE ERA OF HOMELAND SECURITY

Some argue that racial profiling is an absolute necessity given the current terrorist threats facing the United States. Proponents of this particular position argue that if one considers the 9/11 attackers, they were all individuals of Middle Eastern descent, thus, fitting a racial and ethnic profile that if appropriately considered would have prevented these attacks. They further argue that we should have in place, at airports and train stations alike, intelligent systems that consider the race and ethnicity of an individual as a factor when identifying possible terrorists. Although some of you may feel this position is a bit extreme, these mechanisms, as we have learned in previous chapters, are already in place and are being used in order to determine potential terrorists.

Those that argue against racial profiling during the war on terror hold that this is not a very useful tool when attempting to identify potential terrorists. Specifically, they believe that not all terrorists are of the same ethnic and racial composition and thus it is fruitless to attempt to identify terrorists based on this criterion. Further, they argue that if we had such a system in place across the board, it would actually empower terrorist groups such as al-Qaeda as these would simply strive to recruit Caucasian individuals who would be wiling to engage in terrorist activities and would not fit the racial profile in place. Advocates of this position cite instances where individuals who are Caucasian and were born in the United States have engaged in terrorist activities (e.g. Oklahoma City bombing) where a preventive mechanism using racial profiling would have been useless.

The other dimension to consider relates to the civil rights debate. That is, as discussed in previous chapters, civil rights advocates have expressed a strong disapproval regarding the manner in which racial profiling has been used as an alleged weapon in the war on terror. They have filed lawsuits in courts across the United States in an attempt to declare these antiterrorist tactics as illegal and irresponsible. However, others have simply called these allegations "nonsense" as they have cited a true need for us to sacrifice some of our civil rights for the sake of protecting the homeland. Apparently, part of the argument is that we should abandon some of our constitutional rights for the sake of safety. This includes the suspension of our right not to be profiled based on race, ethnicity, gender, or religious affiliation.

Interestingly, the federal government has abolished racial profiling as mandated by former president Bill Clinton during his tenure. However, during the war on terror, the Department of Justice frequently encourages local law enforcement officials to identify and contact individuals whose religious or ethnic background makes them "interesting" sources of information. This is in direct contrast to the philosophy and perspective held by many local law enforcement agencies, which simply ignore the directives of the federal government in this regard (as seen by a police chief's comment in Chapter 7).

FUTURE DIRECTION OF RACIAL PROFILING

It is evident that the future direction of racial profiling is uncertain. With so many dimensions, it is hard to imagine that it will disappear or simply abandon the public's attention. The debates across the nation will continue to press on while not necessarily introducing anything new to this issue. Most of the debates will likely center on the mechanisms used to measure this particular issue. That is, some will continue to argue that we can determine racial profiling practices by collecting data on traffic contacts between police officers and the public. Others, however, will argue that racial profiling is a complex issue that cannot be measured, in its entirety, by traffic contacts. The information to be collected during such contacts will also emerge as a topic of interest. Some will contend that we must record the nature and disposition of all contacts, including the type of searches conducted and the type of contraband collected (if any). Others, however, will continue to argue that most of this data is simply useless as it fails to acknowledge the officer's predisposition to make the stop, or perform the search or arrest.

The collection of data is intrinsically related to the legal standards established by the courts. It is likely that in the coming years, courts will continue to take on the issue of racial profiling, but this time, with more specificity. Courts will likely provide standards for the collection and analysis of data but more specifically issue direction as to how racial profiling should be determined in court. Although most of us will agree that courts will not take a definitive stance regarding racial profiling, it will likely serve us well to have legal standards that academics and practitioners alike can use when studying racial profiling.

Along with the legal changes, we can expect legislative bodies across the United States to continue to enact laws related to racial profiling. Although most of them will probably not agree with one another as to the information to be collected during a traffic stop, they will continue to press for accountability on behalf of law enforcement agencies. Particularly, law enforcement agencies will be asked to put down policies banning racial profiling, while following disciplinary processes as evidence that officers engaging in racism will be punished accordingly.

This issue may also be taken up by the U.S. Congress, and legislation with requirements similar to those currently relevant to the Uniform Crime Report could be passed. It is widely believed that the federal government had plans to enact such legislation prior to 9/11, but given the terrorist attacks and the consequent paradigm shift, this was no longer an immediate priority.

The existing dilemmas regarding racial profiling will also continue to challenge many different groups in society. The public, law enforcement agencies, civil rights advocates, and academics alike are all likely to continue to consider the issue of racial profiling from their own individual perspectives. Given the relatively recent civil rights history in the United States, it is likely that this debate will be passionate and filled with emotions. It is clear, from the vantage point of a social scientist, that we are at a turning point in the history of the world. Given the changes since the 1980s due to the fall of the Iron Curtain and the new political dimensions that have emerged, the United States finds itself at a turning point in the history of humanity in which every move counts and determines the role of this great nation in future endeavors. While this is a global dimension, internally, the United States faces challenges from its own people attempting to redefine the socially acceptable norms that define the character of Americans. Racial profiling is an issue that is likely to remain a challenge in the American society in political, social, and ethical dimensions. We should remain optimistic that although no immediate solutions will likely emerge, consensus will be achieved as to the manner in which we should address this important issue. It is our responsibility, and our call in history to work together to study and address the racial profiling paradox in the near and distant future.

Index